THE CHINESE
GOURMET

THE CHINESE GOURMET

Madame Chin Hau

Edited by Margaret Leeming

BONANZA BOOKS
New York

Contents

Editor's note

The Chinese Gourmet was first written in Chinese and published in Taiwan. Many of the recipes in this English-language edition are direct adaptations of the originals. But in others changes have had inevitably to be made to the ingredients used in the original recipes, where they are difficult or impossible to obtain in the West. This was particularly so in the case of fish, where species differ from region to region throughout the world. Every care has been taken to propose easily available alternatives whilst retaining the original character of the dishes. All the photographs are of dishes cooked with the authentic Chinese ingredients and the written Chinese characters relate to the original dishes.

Servings

Quantities given in the recipes are for 6 average Chinese servings, but in Chinese meals much depends on how many different dishes are being served, so you may wish to increase – or decrease – accordingly.

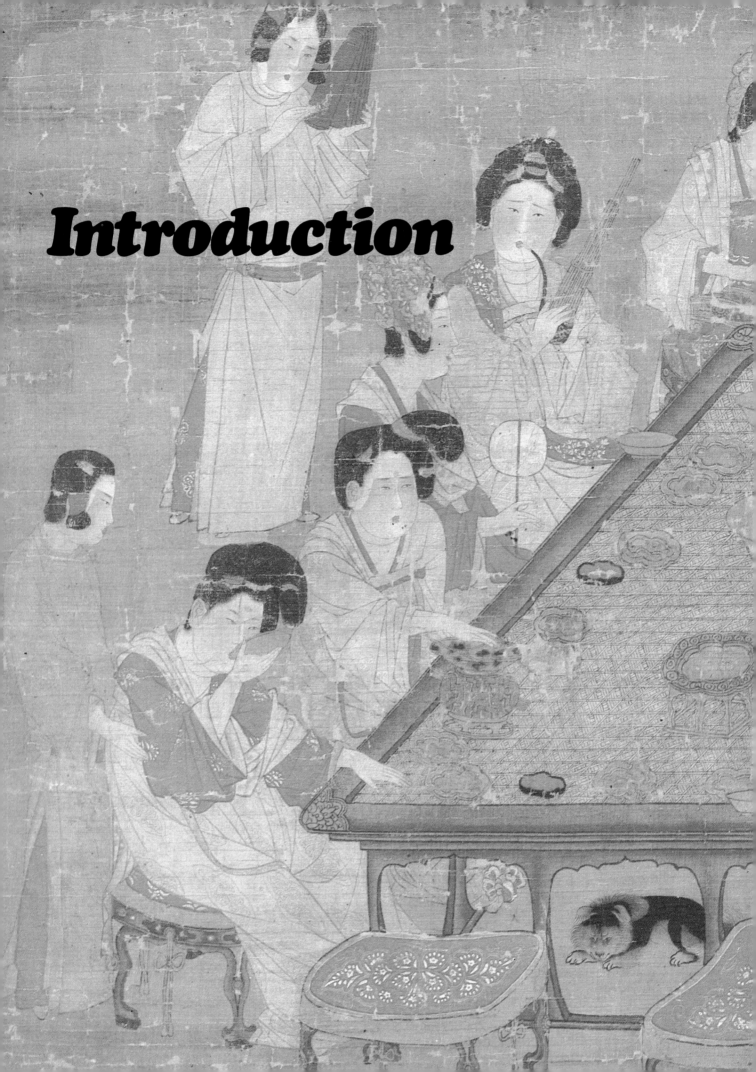

Introduction

Chinese Cuisine in Chinese Paintings

Chinese food has had five thousand years of history. Records show that the Chinese began to use chopsticks in the period of the 'Warring States' (403-222 BC). Food which is not cut up would of course be very difficult to eat at all with chopsticks, and one of the maxims of the great teacher Confucius was 'Eat no food which is not cut properly': such was the importance of proportion in (and appearance of) Chinese food.

The scenes of ancient China depicted in the paintings on the pages that follow show different aspects of cooking, selling food and eating, the latter always a convivial activity.

Cooking, Han Dynasty. Tile from Sichuan (National Historical Museum, Taiwan)

Drinking, chatting and reciting poetry at a feast, Han Dynasty. Tile from Sichuan (National Historical Museum, Taiwan)

Drinking in Lan Pavilion, Song Dynasty, by Guo Zhongshu (10th century)
(National Palace Museum, Taiwan)

Banquet for men of letters, hosted by Emperor Hui Zong, Song Dynasty (12th century). Detail.
(National Palace Museum, Taiwan)

Eighteen scholars climbing Yingzhou mountain, by
Qiu Ying, Ming Dynasty (AD 1494-1552)

Feast in Peach and Plum Garden on a spring night, by Leng Mei (1703-18), Qing Dynasty
(National Palace Museum, Taiwan)

Selling bean milk, by Yao Wenhan (18th century), Qing Dynasty (National Palace Museum,
Taiwan)

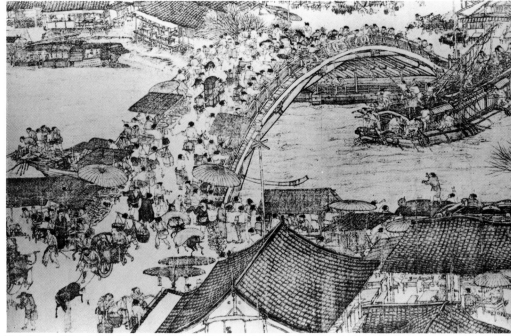

Detail from 'Qing Ming Shang He Tu', by Zhang Zeduan (11th century), Song Dynasty

A family get-together at Chinese New Year: children play in a garden, women cook and old people chat in the living room. By Yao Wenhan (18th century), Qing Dynasty (National Palace Museum, Taiwan)

Guide to Ingredients

Agar-agar: a transparent, colourless dried seaweed used as a vegetarian gelatine. It needs soaking in water before use. Sold in skeins.

Baby corn: tiny corn cobs, sold canned.

Bamboo shoots: the young shoots of bamboo, sold canned in the West. Once opened they can be kept by re-boiling in fresh water every 2-3 days and storing in a clean container in the refrigerator.

Barbecue sauce or **sweet bean sauce:** a sweet savoury sauce made from soya beans and sugar.

Beancurd: a fresh, creamy curd made from soya beans. It has little flavour of its own but goes well with many foods. Sold in squares of varying weights. Keep for up to 4 days, under water in the refrigerator. Change the water each day.

Beancurd skin: brittle sheets of the dried skin which forms on boiling soya bean milk. Dampen to soften before using.

Beansprouts: the young shoots grown from mung or soya beans. Sold fresh in packets.

Black beans: fermented soya or black beans with a strong salty flavour. Sold in bags, or in cans as black beans in salty sauce.

Black dates: a variety of the Chinese jujube with a rather ambiguous flavour. They need soaking for at least 3 hours and slow cooking. Sold dried.

Black fungus: see **wood ears**

Black hair: a black hair-like fungus which needs soaking for 30 minutes in warm water. Sold in small quantities (it is very expensive).

Bok choi: see **cabbage**

Cabbage: there are many different varieties of Chinese cabbage, among them
　choisam, with small bright green leaves, green stalks and yellow flowers;
　bok choi, with white thick stalks all joined at the base and darker green leaves;
　gailan choi, with white flowers and soft green leaves.

Cantonese roast ducks: the shiny, golden brown ducks sometimes seen hanging in Chinese cooked-meat shops. The skin and meat have a sweet, spicy flavour.

Cantonese roast pork or **chahsiu:** has a spicy smell and is golden brown in colour. Sold fresh, chopped into slices, in Chinese cooked-meat shops.

Chahsiu: see **Cantonese roast pork**

Chilli-bean sauce: a very hot, thick sauce made from black beans and chillis with garlic. Sold in jars.

Chinese leaves: a long, solid cabbage looking rather like a cos lettuce. Widely sold in Western markets.

Chinese medlar or **kouchi:** tiny red fruits which have a rough, sweet taste. Sold mainly for medicinal purposes, they are expensive.

Choisam: see **cabbage**

Cinnamon sticks: round smooth sticks of rolled cinnamon bark; they have a milder flavour than powdered cinnamon.

Coriander: a pungent green herb, looking rather like parsley. Sold fresh in bunches.

Crystallized red dates: the fruit of the Chinese jujube, they are prepared with sugar, stoned and ready for eating.

Crystal sugar or rock sugar: rather less sweet than refined Western sugar, it gives a syrupy consistency to sauces.

Dried chestnuts: require soaking in cold water for 24 hours and then simmering in fresh water for 20 minutes before use.

Dried orange peel: made from the skins of Chinese oranges, which in flavour resemble tangerines. A small square of the dried peel gives a delightful tang to savoury stews.

Dried mushrooms: a common ingredient in Chinese cooking, they have a delicate flavour which enhances any savoury dish. Soak in warm water for 30 minutes and use only the caps. Sold by weight, they are expensive.

Dried shrimps: these shrimps will give a lift to the flavour of any savoury dish. Put into hot water and boil for 2 minutes, then leave to soak for 15 minutes *or* soak for 30 minutes in half rice wine, half warm water.

Dried squid: a delicacy in Chinese cooking, with a sweet taste and resilient texture. The squid are cleaned and opened flat before drying. (See page 23 for preparation and cutting.)

Fermented black beans: *see* **black beans**

Fish balls: commercially-made fish balls are sold fresh in Chinese grocers. Buy only when required for immediate use.

Five-spice powder, or **wuxiang:** a sweet mixture of powdered spices, used in small quantities in savoury Chinese dishes.

Fried beancurd: deep-fried squares of beancurd sold ready processed in Chinese grocers. Keep in the refrigerator for up to a week.

Gailan choi: *see* **cabbage**

Ginger: fresh root ginger is used extensively as a flavouring in Chinese cooking. Buy firm, shiny-skinned roots. Powdered ginger is not a satisfactory substitute.

Gingko nuts: fleshy nuts without any strong natural flavour, they blend in well with other foods. Sold only in cans in the West, often labelled 'white nuts'.

Glutinous rice: a round-grained rice with a high gluten content; very sticky when cooked. Wash and soak for at least an hour before cooking.

Glutinous rice flour: finely ground glutinous rice used for making rice balls.

Hoisin sauce: a Cantonese bean sauce made with soya beans, sugar and vinegar. Used as a dip and for flavouring Cantonese roast pork.

Jellyfish: salted, and flaccid to the touch, when prepared jellyfish has a delightful crunchy texture. Pour boiling water over the flat sheets, then soak in cold water for 3 days. Change the water each day.

Kelp: *see* **seaweed**

Kouchi: *see* **Chinese medlar**

Lily buds: the dried flower buds of a tiger-lily, light brown in colour and with a pleasant, slightly acrid flavour. Soak in hot water for 30 minutes before using. Traditionally they are tied before cooking with a single knot in the centre of each. Sold in packets.

Lotus leaves: the dried leaves of the water-lily, they should be soaked in boiling water until they are soft and pliable. Sold in bundles.

Lotus root: the large rhizomes of the water-lily are sometimes sold fresh in Chinese grocers in the West. Also sold cut and par-boiled in cans.

Maltose: a sugar syrup made from wheat starch. Substitute honey.

Mung beans: small dried green beans used for making green-bean paste and for growing beansprouts. Soak overnight before cooking.

Nori: *see* **seaweed**

Oyster sauce: an appetising, unctuous sauce used to add flavour to green vegetables and other dishes. Sold in bottles.

Pea-starch noodles: *see* **silk noodles.** (Also known as **bean vermicelli.**)

Pickled mustard greens: salt pickled cabbage with a sour flavour, usually sold in cans. Rinse well before using. Once opened the keeping life is limited.

Pine kernels, pine nuts: small, slightly aromatic nuts used in cooked dishes. Sold in Western healthfood shops.

Prawns: prawns in the West are sold either raw, unshelled and frozen, and grey in colour; or cooked, with or without their shells, fresh or frozen, and pink. The recipes specify where necessary the variety required.

Quails' eggs: tiny eggs with a delicate flavour, often used whole in Chinese cooking. Sold in delicatessens.

Red beancurd: beancurd processed with the lees of wine. It has a strong, salty, rather sharp flavour. Sold in jars or cans.

Red beans: small dried adzuki beans used to make red-bean paste. Soak overnight before cooking.

Red dates: the dried red fruits of the Chinese jujube. Soak for at least 3 hours before cooking. Remove the stones either before or after cooking.

Red-in-snow: a winter cabbage always sold salted. Sold in cans in the West, often labelled 'snow-cabbage' or sometimes 'pickled cabbage'.

Rice: Long-grained rice is the standard southern Chinese rice, although a variety of short-grained rice, similar to American Rose, is also eaten. Wash the rice well, then cook with water in the proportion 5 rice to 6 water (volume measures). Bring the water to the boil with the rice, cover the pan and cook over a moderate heat until the water has gone (about 15 minutes). Then lower the heat and cook, closely covered, for another 10 minutes. Finally turn off the heat and leave, still with the lid on, for another 15 minutes.

Rice cakes: made from the crust of dry cooked rice. Boil long-grain rice in the normal manner but continue cooking for at least 15 minutes longer than usual to allow a dry crust to form round the pan, without browning. Scoop out any soft loose rice and pour in about 15ml (1 tablespoon) oil, round the edge of the pan. Heat gently for a few minutes, then loosen the rice crust with a spatula. Turn out on to a plate. This may now be stored (preferably frozen) until required. If stored in a deep-freeze, it will need de-frosting and drying in a moderate oven for 5 minutes before use.

Rice wine: see **wine**

Salted eggs: raw ducks' eggs preserved in brine. Sold coated in dry soot. Wash carefully before use.

Sausages: many varieties of Chinese sausages are on sale, the most usual variety being made with pork or liver and resembling a thin salami.

Sea cucumbers: sea slugs, sold dried, in various sizes, the bigger the more expensive. Soak in cold water for 3 days, changing the water every day. Then boil for 20 minutes in fresh water. Scrub thoroughly on the outside and slit down to clean the insides. When clean, put into chicken stock and simmer for an hour. Discard this stock and use the sea cucumbers as directed.

Seaweed:

   kelp comes in long, dried strips. To use as a salad boil for 10 minutes, then wash well. To use for a vegetarian stock do *not* boil, only simmer, or the stock will be bitter.

   nori: a processed form of laver seaweed. Thin sheets of Japanese *nori* can be toasted and eaten as an appetizer. (The Chinese variety of this seaweed is coarser and cannot be eaten without proper cooking.)

Sesame oil: a delicate oil extracted from sesame seeds. Used as a final seasoning for many stir-fried dishes. If used for frying take care not to overheat, for the flavour is destroyed by high temperatures.

Shachajiang: a southern savoury sauce used as a dip for a fire-pot. It contains shrimps, dried fish, spices and rice flour.

Sichuan peppercorns: the native Chinese pepper, which is more spicy than hot. The dried calyx and seeds look rather like brown cloves.

Sichuan preserved vegetable: the peppery club stalk of a variety of Chinese cabbage preserved with hot spices. Sold in cans. When opened remove from can and store covered in the refrigerator. It will keep for months. Rinse before using.

Silk noodles: also known as pea-starch noodles, or bean vermicelli, made from mung beans. These wiry, transparent noodles need soaking in very hot water for 10 minutes before use.

Silver ears: dried white, almost transparent fungus used in both sweet and savoury dishes. Soak in hot water for 30 minutes, then rinse thoroughly and trim. Sold in packets, it is expensive in the West.

Snow peas: see **sugar peas**

Soy sauce: the basic Chinese flavouring sauce, sold in bottles in both Chinese grocers and Western supermarkets. Soy sauce made in China is labelled *'superior soy'* for a lighter, saltier variety and *'soy, superior sauce'* for a heavier, rich-flavoured soy.

Spring roll skins: large squares of thin pasta made from wheat flour, sold ready made in Chinese stores. The fresh variety is better than the frozen.

Star anise: the star-shaped dried brown calyx and seeds of the anise plant have a strong aniseed flavour. Use in small quantities.

Straw mushrooms: delicate ball-shaped mushrooms with a faint woodland flavour. They are grown on straw, hence their name. Occasionally sold fresh, more often canned, in the West.

Sugar peas: delicate-flavoured peas eaten whole with their pods.

Sweet bean sauce: see **barbecue sauce**

Sweet potato: sometimes known as the Louisiana yam, the best varieties have a purplish skin and yellow flesh. Sold fresh in ethnic markets.

Tianjin pickled cabbage: a dry pickled cabbage with a sweetish flavour, sometimes with garlic added. It needs no preparation before cooking.

Vinegar: Chinese vinegar, usually made from rice, has a gentle flavour lacking the astringency often associated with malt vinegars. Black and white are available. Red vinegar, made from sorghum, has a spicy flavour rather similar to Worcestershire sauce.

Water chestnuts: the crunchy tubers of an aquatic plant, sometimes sold fresh in the West. If fresh, peel and keep under water to prevent browning before use. Also sold canned, it can be stored in a deep-freeze after opening.

White radish: a long white root vegetable resembling an overgrown white carrot. Sold in supermarkets in the West under the name Dutch rettish.

Wine (rice wine): made from glutinous rice, this is a rather coarse weak spirit, about 16° proof, used everywhere in China for cooking. It may also be drunk, warmed and slightly sweetened with sugar to taste.

Winter melon: a large green-skinned gourd, sometimes known in the West as a wax gourd, weighing up to 4kg (8 lb). Usually sold canned in the West.

Wood ears or **black fungus:** the biggest and thickest variety of dried black fungi sold in the West. They are black on one side and light grey with a slight bloom on the other. Soak for 30 minutes in warm water, then rinse well and trim.

Wuntun skins: small squares of thin pasta sold ready-made in packets of 30 from Chinese grocers; they are used for making dumplings and *wuntun*.

Wuxiang: see **five-spice powder**

Yam: see **sweet potato**

Youtiao: deep-fried batter sticks, about 20cm (8 inches) long, sold ready-made in Chinese grocers.

Cutting Food for Chinese Dishes

In the preparation of Chinese food cutting is as important as cooking. The way the food is cut affects the taste as well as the appearance of the dish.

6. Tenderize the meat by beating it with the cleaver.
7. Slice in half lengthwise.
8. Cut diagonally into small pieces.

To cut pork shreds:
1. After removing the membranes and fat, slice thinly.
2. Cut the thin slices into small strips or shreds.

Pork
1. Remove any membranes.
2. Remove any fat.
3. Cut through the meat to open out into a flat sheet.
4. Cut through a second time
5. Open out to make one large thin sheet of meat.

Chicken
1. Cut off the bottoms of the legs.
2. Slit down the back of the chicken.
3,4. Turn the chicken over and cut down alongside the breast bone on each side.
5. Pull off the meat from the breast, cutting free where necessary.

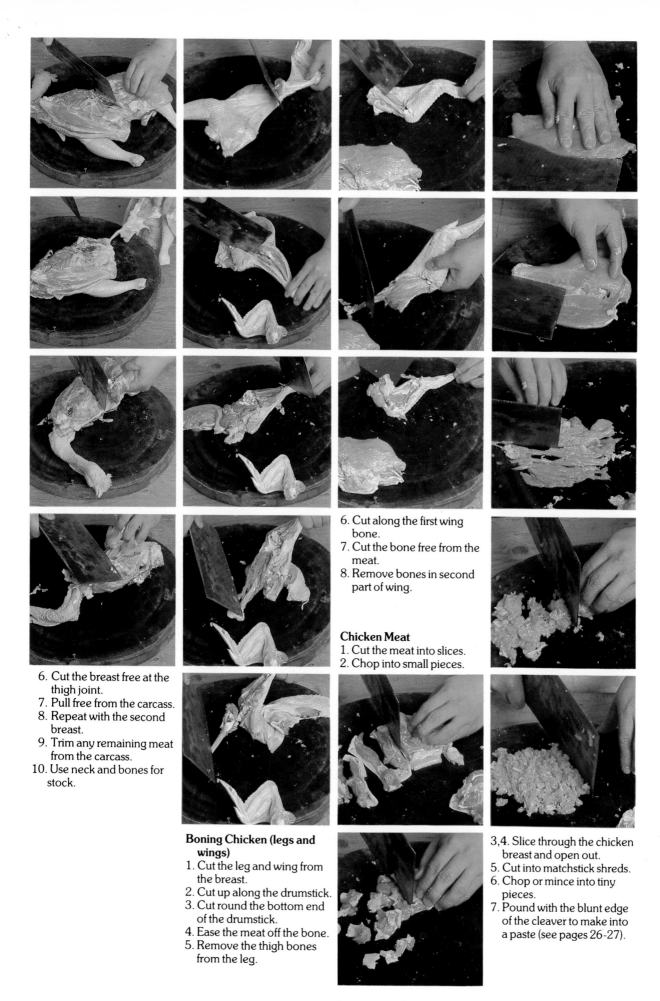

6. Cut the breast free at the thigh joint.
7. Pull free from the carcass.
8. Repeat with the second breast.
9. Trim any remaining meat from the carcass.
10. Use neck and bones for stock.

6. Cut along the first wing bone.
7. Cut the bone free from the meat.
8. Remove bones in second part of wing.

Chicken Meat
1. Cut the meat into slices.
2. Chop into small pieces.

Boning Chicken (legs and wings)
1. Cut the leg and wing from the breast.
2. Cut up along the drumstick.
3. Cut round the bottom end of the drumstick.
4. Ease the meat off the bone.
5. Remove the thigh bones from the leg.

3,4. Slice through the chicken breast and open out.
5. Cut into matchstick shreds.
6. Chop or mince into tiny pieces.
7. Pound with the blunt edge of the cleaver to make into a paste (see pages 26-27).

21

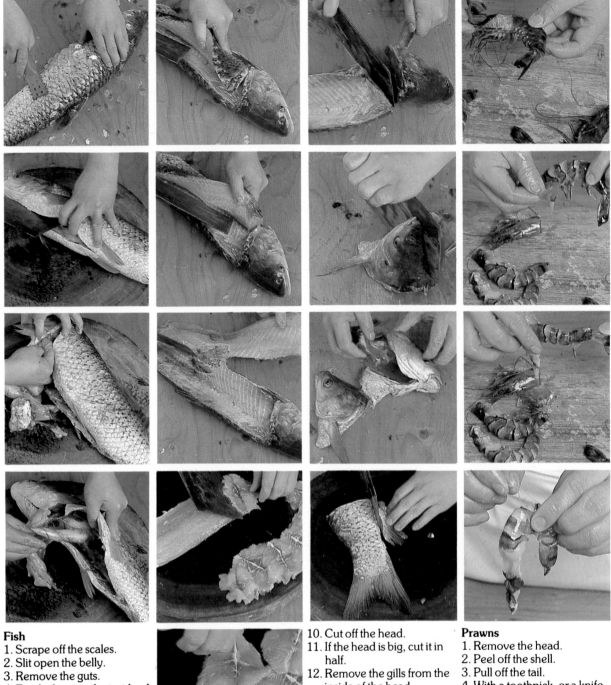

Fish
1. Scrape off the scales.
2. Slit open the belly.
3. Remove the guts.
4. Finish cleaning the inside of the fish and rinse well in cold water.

5,6,7. Slice along the fish's backbone, then cut the top fillet free. Repeat on the other side.

8,9. Take one fillet, skin-side-down, and slice thinly down to the skin in a V-shaped pattern, leaving each slice attached to the fillet.

10. Cut off the head.
11. If the head is big, cut it in half.
12. Remove the gills from the inside of the head.
13. Slice a tail piece of fish lengthwise into two. Trim off the fins.

Prawns
1. Remove the head.
2. Peel off the shell.
3. Pull off the tail.
4. With a toothpick, or a knife, remove the black digestive cord which runs through the centre of the body.

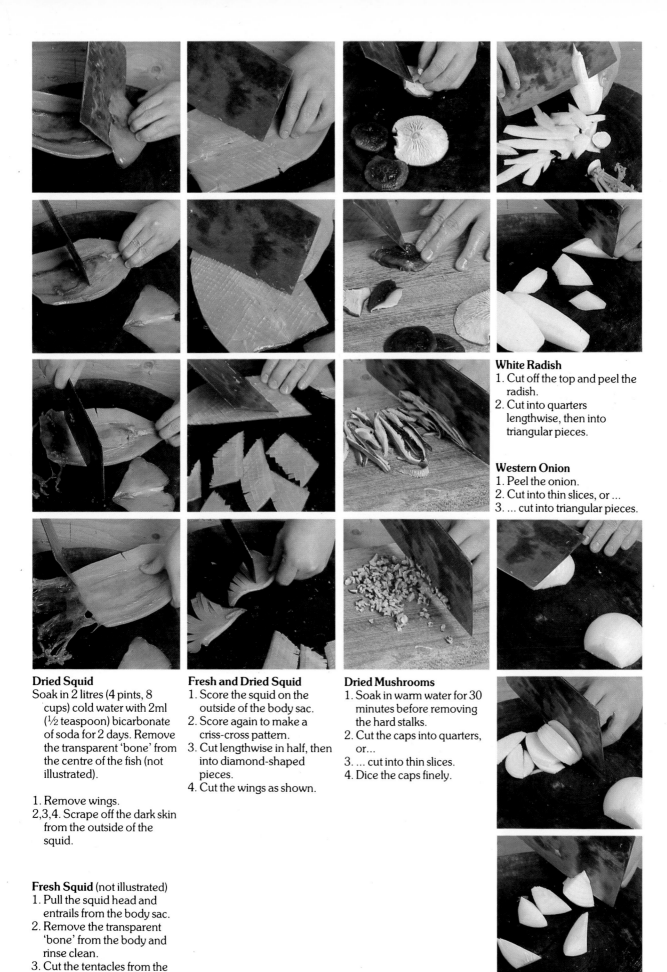

Dried Squid

Soak in 2 litres (4 pints, 8 cups) cold water with 2ml (½ teaspoon) bicarbonate of soda for 2 days. Remove the transparent 'bone' from the centre of the fish (not illustrated).

1. Remove wings.
2,3,4. Scrape off the dark skin from the outside of the squid.

Fresh Squid (not illustrated)

1. Pull the squid head and entrails from the body sac.
2. Remove the transparent 'bone' from the body and rinse clean.
3. Cut the tentacles from the head above the eyes and reserve.
4. Skin the tentacles and body sac.

Fresh and Dried Squid

1. Score the squid on the outside of the body sac.
2. Score again to make a criss-cross pattern.
3. Cut lengthwise in half, then into diamond-shaped pieces.
4. Cut the wings as shown.

Dried Mushrooms

1. Soak in warm water for 30 minutes before removing the hard stalks.
2. Cut the caps into quarters, or...
3. ... cut into thin slices.
4. Dice the caps finely.

White Radish

1. Cut off the top and peel the radish.
2. Cut into quarters lengthwise, then into triangular pieces.

Western Onion

1. Peel the onion.
2. Cut into thin slices, or ...
3. ... cut into triangular pieces.

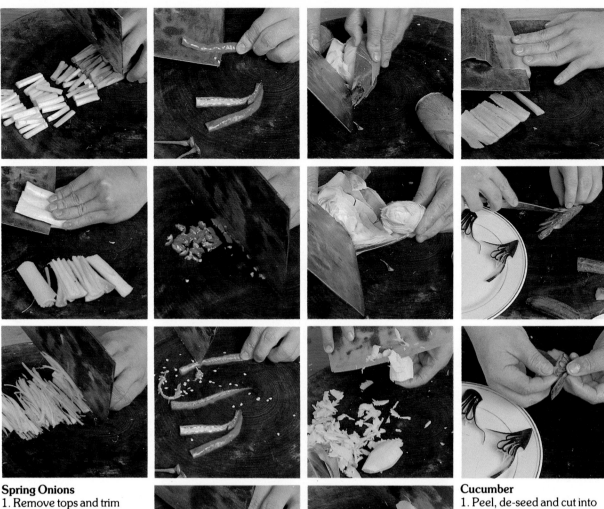

Spring Onions
1. Remove tops and trim ends. Cut the onions into sections.
2. Cut the sections into halves.
3. Shred sections lengthwise.

Chillis
1. Cut off the top and slice the chilli in half.
2. Chop the chilli into small pieces. (The seeds left in will make the dish hotter.)
3,4. De-seed the chilli and cut slantwise into pieces.

Fresh Bamboo Shoots
1,2,3. Peeling a fresh bamboo shoot.
4. Slicing fresh or canned bamboo shoots.

Cucumber
1. Peel, de-seed and cut into short batons.
2,3. Make cucumber garnishes by cutting the cucumber in half lengthwise, then cutting nicks of equal lengths down each side. Fold in, as shown, to shape.

White Radish/Carrot Flowers
Soak for 2 hours. Cut into short lengths, carve to form the petals and dye as required.

Tomato Lilies
Cut the tomato into 6 segments. Pare off the skin to half-way down each segment and bend away from the flesh. Re-assemble as a lily flower.

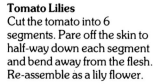

24

Using cutting dies for white radish.

Conversion table for fluid measures

Metric	Imperial	US
5 ml	1 teaspoon	1 teaspoon
15ml	1 tablespoon	1 tablespoon
120ml	4 fl oz	½ cup
150ml	¼ pint	⅔ cup
225ml	8 fl oz	1 cup
300ml	½ pint	1¼ cups
450ml	¾ pint	2 cups
600ml	1 pint	2½ cups
750ml	24 fl oz	3 cups

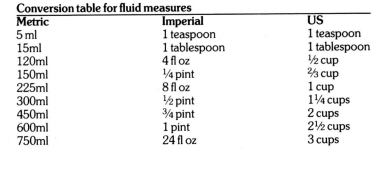

Flower Basket

1. Cut the white onion sections into brushes and fasten a ring of chilli round each.
2. Slash the chillis into flower shapes.
3. Scoop out the flesh from half a tomato to make a basket, and arrange onion, chilli and parsley in it, or ...
4. ... carve a basket from a green pepper and fill with the prepared 'flowers'.

Chinese cooking methods

Marinating

Meat, poultry, fish and vegetables need cutting into suitable-sized pieces for the dish (pages 20-4) and then, very often, are left to marinate for a while before being cooked. Marinating tenderizes, improves flavour and, in addition, provides a film of starch which protects the tissues against hot oil, and in some cases it reduces strong flavours. The ingredients of marinades vary according to the recipe, and can be very elaborate. At their simplest they usually include soy sauce, rice wine, cornflour and salt, or a selection of these, but they may also contain spring onions, ginger, spices and special flavouring sauces. Small pieces of meat or fish require only 30 minutes' marinating, but large pieces of meat and whole birds may need up to twelve hours.

Preparing Meat Pastes

In addition to chopping and mincing meat (page 21, *Chicken Meat*, step 6), it is sometimes necessary to pound it into a paste to be used for meatballs or a dumpling stuffing. After the meat has been cut and pounded with the blunt edge of a cleaver (step 7), fold it over on top of itself and pound across at right angles to the previous movement. Continue pounding and from time to time sprinkle over a little cold water or rice wine: 45ml (3 tablespoons) to 275g (9 oz) meat. When the meat pulp is smooth and almost creamy, use as required.

Cooking Pans

The Chinese use a deep, curved-bottom pan called a wok for almost all kinds of cooking. It is possible to create deep-frying conditions in a wok with only a cupful of oil, then, after pouring out all but a tablespoon or so of oil, to continue stir-frying in the same pan. Covered with a domed lid, the wok can be used for slow simmering, while a trivet or steaming basket converts it into an excellent steamer. The rounded bottom of the wok fits into the traditional Chinese stove, providing direct contact with the source of the heat to half-way up the sides of the pan. This allows a very high temperature to be built up in the centre of the pan. However, flat-topped Western hobs present serious problems. A gas cooker, using a special ring to hold the wok steady, will produce reasonable results, although always at a lower temperature than is ideal, but an electric cooker never has enough contact with the surface of a wok to attain the required level of heat. It is now possible to buy flat-bottomed woks which will go some way to solving this problem, but they should never be used for deep-frying. A heavy paella pan makes an excellent substitute for a wok for stir-frying on an electric hob, or even a large Western frying-pan. For deep-fat frying under Western conditions it is probably better to use a deep-fat pan with a fine mesh basket and then transfer to a wok or other pan.

Stir-frying

This is probably the most commonly used Chinese cooking technique; stir-frying depends on continual movement of the food round the pan while it is cooking. Food for stir-fried dishes should remain moist and firm when cooked, and the dish as a whole should be dry, not greasy. Heat control is the main factor in achieving such results. The cooking must be done at as high a temperature as possible without actually burning the food. This is best controlled by lifting and lowering the pan over the fire during the cooking, while keeping the source of heat at its maximum.

Heat the pan before adding the oil, to prevent food sticking to the pan. Put in the seasonings – such as chopped onion and ginger – and stir-fry for about 15 seconds before adding the main ingredients. Then stir-fry very quickly over a high heat. The food should have been cut into shreds or thin slices before you start cooking, so that it will cook very quickly. Add a final touch of soy sauce and serve immediately the cooking is finished.

Deep-frying

This method of cooking is more usually one among others in the preparation of a dish than the main cooking method. To deep-fry there should be enough oil in the pan to cover the food to twice its depth. Heat the oil to very hot, add the food, then lower the heat and fry until the food is cooked through, or over a high heat quickly cook the food until it is crisp on the outside. Food fried over a high temperature has usually already been cooked, or will be cooked again by another method.

Braising

This method of cooking is very similar to stir-frying and uses the stir-frying action in the beginning; however, the cooking process as a whole takes longer, and the food may therefore be cut into bigger pieces. Braising differs from stir-frying in that after the initial frying a seasoning sauce is added and the food is cooked in this sauce for a while until done. A wide range of seasonings is used in braising sauces, which can create sophisticated flavours in a dish – such as sweet and sour, or fish-fragrant. Before the braise is served the sauce is usually thickened with cornflour or some other thickening agent.

Steaming

This is probably one of the oldest forms of Chinese cooking. It has a great advantage over other methods because food cooked in steam retains its original shape and the flavour remains fresh and natural. A Chinese steamer is made of circular boxes of bamboo with lattice-work bottoms, each section fitting firmly on to the rim of another; the top box is covered by a domed woven bamboo lid. The bowls or plates of food are put uncovered into separate sections of the steamer and the whole edifice placed on top of a wok filled with boiling water. Alternatively a plate or bowl can be stood on a trivet in a wok containing water; the water should come to just 2cm (1 inch) below the level of the stand, and the wok covered by its lid. A Western steamer can of course be substituted. Which ever method you use, take care the pan does not boil dry. Most steamed foods are cooked in their marinades.

Poaching or Boiling

This method of cooking covers several different kinds of dishes. Already seasoned and partly or completely cooked ingredients for soups are united in boiling stock or water, then cooked for a short time together before being served; in fire-pots, unseasoned thinly-sliced foods are dipped in boiling water or stock until cooked, then seasoned and eaten; while for other dishes larger pieces of food are simply boiled in water before being cooled and seasoned with an additional sauce. These are usually served cold.

Stewing

There are two kinds of Chinese stews. One, in which lightly seasoned food is cooked in water or stock in a *bain-marie*, produces a clear, light-coloured, delicate gravy, and the food retains its shape. This process is very similar to slow steaming. In the other method of stewing the pot is put directly on to the heat and the food is cooked in a stock seasoned with soy sauce and sugar, often together with sweet spices such as five-spice, cinnamon or star anise. It is cooked for a long time over a low heat, allowing the food to absorb the flavours of the stock. The final gravy is dark-coloured and thick, and this kind of dish is often called 'red-cooked'.

Oven Cooking

Ovens are not common in Chinese domestic kitchens. Most oven-cooked dishes, such as Peking Duck, are cooked only in restaurants. When using a Western oven to roast poultry or meat Chinese-style it should be hung from the top bars of the oven and a drip tray placed underneath, so that the heat can reach all sides of the meat evenly. The flavour will often be improved by basting from time to time during cooking with a seasoning sauce. An oven can be used to smoke food in a closed roasting tin, although this can also be done on top of the hob in a heavy pot lined with tinfoil. Heat the smoking materials (tea, sugar, rice, for example) until they start to smoke vigorously, then stand the food to be smoked on a rack above them. Cover the pot or roasting tin very closely and allow to smoke for about 10 minutes. Note that smoking is not intended to cook the food, only to flavour it.

Pickling

This process is intended to give either raw or cooked foods a distinctive flavour. Cooked chicken may be soaked in wine, as in Drunken Chicken; raw vegetables in a brine solution (for several days), as in Sichuan Pickled Vegetables. Both result in special textures and tastes. The pickling procedure is not a method of preserving, however.

Wind Drying

Hanging foods (sausages and other meats, for example) in a dry, airy place gives them a unique flavour and also helps to preserve them. However, the process depends entirely on a long period of dry, windy weather.

Recipes Listed by Cooking Methods

Regional Styles of Cooking

China is a vast country of a thousand million people stretching from the steppes of Inner Mongolia to the sub-tropical forests of Hainan and Guangxi. Chinese cooking reflects the range and diversity of the land and its produce as well as the different historical experiences of the various regions. The regional cooking styles of China can roughly be divided into the four points of the compass, but within each area there are often wide variations in local cuisine. Generally speaking, the largest centres of population have produced the most famous cuisines.

Northern cooking

This region is dominated by Beijing, which itself has no particular style but inherits the very best of all regions; it is famous for its elaborate and sophisticated dishes, many of which came originally from the imperial palace. The surrounding region has a harsh climate and its food reflects the poverty of the people. *Jiaozi* – boiled dumplings filled with meat and vegetables in a wheat-flour skin – are a basic dish. Noodles or steamed bread are more usual than rice, and the seasonings of garlic, coriander, onion and vinegar are typical of the region.

Western cooking

This region includes Sichuan, Hunan and Yunnan, where a damp, warm climate allows for long growing seasons. The people eat rice and a lot of vegetables. The cuisine of the area is particularly distinguished by the subtle mixture of seasonings employed in any one dish – as in the 'fish-fragrant' sauces – as well as by the fiery heat of the chillis included in many of the region's dishes. Western Chinese season their food generously with Sichuan pepper, chillis, garlic, sesame and vinegar.

Southern cooking

Cantonese cooking has long been the most familiar style of Chinese cuisine in the West. The region covers Guangdong, Guangxi, Fujian and Taiwan, a rich land with mild winters where the farmers can grow a profusion of fruit and green vegetables throughout the year. Rice is the basic staple, and the long shore-line provides an enormous variety of fish and seafood, for which the cuisine of the region is famous. Fujian and Taiwan have a tradition of slow-cooked colourless soups, while other Cantonese specialities include steamed dishes and highly decorated, rather sweet dishes including fruit with the vegetables and meat. The tradition of fine food in Guangdong is enshrined in the Chinese proverb 'Eat in Canton, die in Suzhou' (Suzhou boasts craftsmen famous for the quality of their coffins).

Eastern cooking

The cuisine of this area is based on Shanghai, but it includes Zhejiang and Jiangsu as well as Anhui. This area straddling the Yangzi River grows rice and wheat as well as a wide range of vegetables. Fish, from both fresh-water ponds and the sea, is a major item in eastern food. The cooking styles of the region belong to a very old tradition of Chinese courtly cooking, in which tremendous attention is paid to the details of making stock and cutting food, and to the presentation of food after it has been cooked. One speciality of the area is the slow-cooked stew seasoned with soy sauce and sugar. More oil and more sugar is used in eastern cooking than in other regional styles.

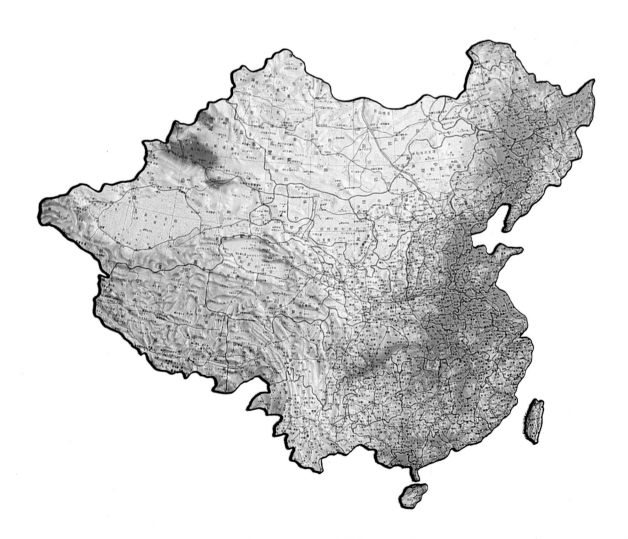

Recipes Listed by Region

Chinese Meals and Menus

The Chinese love big dinners and banquets: for them eating is a form of recreation. A banquet is meant to impress, on two levels: it is an implied compliment to the guests in its lavishness, and it serves to display the wealth and social standing of the host. The guest of honour, or the eldest guest, at a banquet is seated first, furthest from and facing the door, while the other guests take their positions according to their social status around the table. The host sits opposite the senior guest with his back to the door. The courses of the banquet follow a prescribed pattern. Some dishes will be made of expensive ingredients, while others will involve hours of work. A banquet in Pre-Liberation China would have started with sixteen cold *hors d'oeuvres* made up of:

4 dishes of dessert or candies
4 dishes of fresh fruits
4 dishes of dried fruits, including nuts
4 dishes of preserved fruits

These would be removed when all the guests were seated, to be returned later, and would be replaced by:

4 dishes of cold meats

followed by:

2-4 dishes of stir-fried or quickly-cooked foods, all served at the same time
4 large dishes, served separately (these, the main dishes of the banquet, would always include a whole bird, a big pot and a whole fish)
2-4 dessert dishes, usually 2 salty and 2 sweet (these dishes marked the transition between the dishes with which wine was drunk and those accompanied by rice or grain with which no wine was drunk)
6 large dishes to go with rice (simply prepared dishes without elaborate cooking styles, and including at least one soup).

Finally the original fruit dishes might be brought back as a signal that the meal was at an end – it was not, and is not, customary for guests to linger once the food is finished at a Chinese banquet.

A modern banquet, although still containing many dishes, would be much more limited in scale. It would probably consist of:

1 cold plate of cooked mixed meats, usually very elaborately arranged
2 stir-fried dishes
4 big dishes (or more, depending on the number of guests, but including a chicken, a duck, a whole fish and a big pot)
1 dessert (sometimes two sweet dishes together with a small savoury dish)
Rice or noodles (perhaps fried rice and vegetables, or noodles with a meat sauce) followed by:
1 soup.

It is often the custom to serve an ice-cream and perhaps tea either at the end of a big meal or between courses to aid the digestion; also, raw fruit is now often served at the end of a meal. The cooking and serving of such a meal, although it is smaller in scale than the old traditional banquets, involves a tremendous amount of work by several cooks working throughout the meal, and is beyond the scope of most Western housewives in their own homes. The menus given below are graded from very time-consuming banquets requiring hours of work to simple family meals that can be easily prepared in the average Western home.

Most Chinese family meals are planned on the principle of one soup, four main dishes and rice or noodles. The choice of the four dishes depends on personal taste, but they must contain an element of variety in both ingredients and styles of cooking as well as in contrasts of flavour and texture. So pork, chicken, fish and vegetables could all be included in one meal, with beef, mutton, shellfish, eggs and beancurd used to give a wider variety to the dishes. The size of the pieces of food in the dishes can be varied, from bite-sized or shreds to whole birds. Different cooking styles, such as steaming and stewing contrasted with stir-fries and braises, help to lend interest to the meal, while the seasonings can range from bland through sweet and sour to pepper hot. For the Western cook the main difficulty in producing a Chinese meal is in planning a panic-free timetable which ensures that the dishes will all be cooked at the right moment. Unlike much Western cooking, the actual cooking of a Chinese meal takes very little time: it is the preparation which is time-consuming and often involves unfamiliar routines. The golden rule in cooking Chinese is to allow enough time to finish all the preparation of the food before it is due to be cooked, and to choose dishes which will not all require last-minute attention.

Drinks

Many people drink tea with Chinese meals. *Puer*, a black tea, is particularly suitable since it protects the digestion against fatty and rich foods. Oolong, a half-fermented tea, also goes well with food. Both black and half-fermented teas should be made with boiling water. For drinking after the meal a flower tea such as jasmine or a green tea such as Longjing is preferable; these teas should be made with water that is not quite boiling.

If you wish to drink alcohol with the meal *huadiao* is a smoother, matured type of rice wine, slightly stronger than the average Western table wine. It should be warmed and sweetened to taste, and served in very small glasses. The Chinese produce red and white grape wine, but most Westerners would probably prefer to drink a light German, French or Californian Bordeaux-style wine. It is possible to drink spirits with Chinese food: indeed, in Hong Kong and Taiwan it is not uncommon for people to drink brandy or whisky throughout a meal. Otherwise, there is *moutai*, a fearsome white spirit made from millet and wheat, approximately 106° proof and quite famous in the West; there is also a rose-flavoured spirit labelled *mei kuei lu chiew*, which many people find pleasant —though very strong.

Banquet Menus

Menu 1

Plum Blossom Plate	39
Dry-fried Beef Shreds	71
Stir-fried Dried Squid	172
Sweet Congee with Rice Balls	222
Feather-duster Spareribs	58
Steamed Chicken with Broccoli	96
Stir-fried Prawns with Chives	133
'Fish-fragrant' Beef	71
Lohan's Delight	204
Smoked Fish	150
Steamed Winter Melon Soup	195
Four-shreds Spring Rolls	221
Three Coloured Bean Pastes	219

Menu 2

Phoenix Cold Plate	38
Strange-flavoured Chicken	93
Stir-fried Squid with Coriander and Garlic	160
Cantonese Sweet and Sour Pork	43
Shacha (southern fire-pot)	208
Peking Duck	114
Fried Carp	127
'Raw Fish' Soup	143
Hundred-treasures Rice	219
Silver Ears with Pineapple	223

Menu 3

Drunken Chicken	97
Five-colour Shreds	120
Spiced Fish	144
Three-shreds Salad	165
Stir-fried Chicken with Walnuts	90
Sweet and Sour crispy Fish	137
Quail Eggs with Ham and Shrimps	163
Stir-fried Red and Green Peppers	198
Braised Lamb with Red Dates	77
Crispy Fried Chicken	100
Steamed Sweet Ham with Bread	65
Fish Pot	143
Stir-fried Squid with Coriander and Garlic	160
Family Reunion	173
Hundred-treasures Rice	219
Sweet Congee with Rice Balls	222

Family Menus

Menu 1

Sweet and Sour Pork	40
Stir-fried Prawns with Cauliflower	141
Steamed Chicken with Green Onions	119
Stir-fried Red and Green Peppers	198
Cabbage Soup with Meatballs	40

Menu 2

Stir-fried Pork Shreds with Watercress	46
Salted Chicken with Black Beans	116
Scallops and Baby Corn	167
Braised Fish	155
Ham and Corn Soup	56

Menu 3

Dry-fried French Beans	193
Strange-flavoured Chicken	93
Pork with Red Beancurd Sauce	64
Prawns and Broccoli	137
Pork and White Radish Pot	50

Menu 4

Sweet and Sour Vegetables	200
Spiced Chicken Wings	111
Deep-fried Pork with Arrowheads	60
'Fish-fragrant' Omelette	178
Bacon Soup	61

Recipes

Butterfly Cold Plate

蝴蝶拼盤

200g (7 oz) each fish paste (from
 Japanese stores),
 Cantonese roast pork,
 Cantonese roast duck,
 cooked pig's liver (all from
 Chinese cooked meat
 shop), cooked ham
Garnish: carrot, parsley, chilli,
 tomato, glacé cherries

Slice the meats into thin triangles. Arrange them on a plate in the shape of a butterfly. Garnish around the edge with carved carrot, parsley, chilli flowers, tomato flowers, etc.

Three-colour Cold Plate

三色拼盤

Use the same ingredients to make up this cold plate. Arrange and decorate as you wish.

37

Phoenix Cold Plate

彩鳳大拼盤

150g (5 oz) each cooked pig's liver, cooked
   pig's tongue, Cantonese roast pork,
   Cantonese roast duck (all from Chinese
   cooked meat shop), fish roll (from
   Japanese store), cooked ham
2 large dried mushrooms
250g (8 oz) white radish
1 carrot
parsley
glacé cherries

Slice the meats into thin triangles. Soak the mushrooms in hot water until soft. Slice the caps into a fan shape. Shred 30g (1 oz) white radish. Use to form a bed in the centre of the serving plate. Place ham on top of white radish shreds, then arrange tongue, liver pork, duck and fish roll in sequence to look like a phoenix. Cut carrot and remaining white radish into shapes for phoenix tail and wings. Paint with edible food dye and garnish plate with carrot, white radish, parsley and glacé cherries.

Plum Blossom Cold Plate

梅花大拼盤

150g (5 oz) each Chinese sausage, cooked
   pig's liver, cooked pig's tongue, roast duck
   duck and roast pork

Arrange into a plum-blossom shape. Garnish the centre with a carved white radish
flower (see page 24) and some lettuce. Decorate the rim of the plate with slices of
tomato and strips of par-boiled carrot.

Cabbage Soup with Meatballs

白菜肉圓場

300g (10 oz) pork steak	12g (½ oz) dried shrimps
5 water chestnuts	500g (1 lb) Chinese cabbage
10ml (2 teaspoons) salt	2 tomatoes
40ml (2½ tablespoons) rice wine	1 spring onion
15ml (1 tablespoon) light soy sauce	50g (2 oz) spinach
25ml (1½ tablespoons) cornflour	800ml (1⅔ pints, 3½ cups) stock or water

Pound the pork into a paste (see page 26). Mince the water chestnuts and add them together with the salt, 25ml (1½ tablespoons) rice wine, soy sauce and 8ml (½ tablespoon) cornflour to the meat paste. Blend well and shape into 12 balls. Rinse the dried shrimps and soak in 15ml (1 tablespoon) rice wine for 20 minutes. Wash and cut the Chinese cabbage into 5cm (2-inch) squares. Slice the tomatoes. Cut the spring onion into sections. Wash the spinach and cook in boiling water for 5 minutes. Drain well. Mix 15ml (1 tablespoon) cornflour with 30ml (2 tablespoons) water.

Boil the stock or water and add the shrimps, cabbage and spring onion. Season with salt and drop in the meatballs. Remove foam from surface and boil gently until the meat-balls rise to the top (about 5 minutes). Then lift out. Thicken the soup with the cornflour paste and pour into a serving bowl. Arrange tomato slices and spinach in the centre and the meat-balls around the edge of the bowl. Serve.

Sweet and Sour Pork

咕咾肉

450g (1 lb) pork steak	1 spring onion
45ml (3 tablespoons) soy sauce	2 slices ginger
7.5ml (1½ teaspoons) rice wine	5ml (1 teaspoon) salt
75ml (5 tablespoons) cornflour	45ml (3 tablespoons) sugar
2 egg yolks	45ml (3 tablespoons) rice vinegar
12 water chestnuts	oil for deep frying
150g (5 oz) calabrese	

Cut pork into 2cm (1-inch) cubes. Marinate in 20ml (1½ tablespoons) soy sauce, the wine, 7.5ml (1½ teaspoons) cornflour and egg yolks for 1 hour. Roll in 45ml (3 tablespoons) dry cornflour until each piece is well coated. Cut the water chestnuts in halves. Wash the broccoli and tear into florets. Cut the spring onion into sections. Mix 20ml (4 teaspoons) cornflour with 30ml (2 tablespoons) water.

Heat the deep fat and fry the pork cubes for 2 minutes. Lift them out and re-heat the oil. Deep-fry for another minute. Heat a pan with 30ml (2 tablespoons) oil. Stir-fry the onion and ginger, add the broccoli, water chestnuts, and salt. Pour in 25ml (1½ tablespoons) soy sauce, the sugar, vinegar and finally 125ml (4 fl oz, ½ cup) water. Boil gently until broccoli is done and stir in cornflour paste to thicken. Mix in pork cubes and coat evenly with the sauce. Arrange on a plate and serve.

Steamed Pork with Preserved Cabbage

梅菜扣肉

25g (1 oz) dried cabbage	600g (1 lb 5 oz) belly of pork
15 white Chinese cabbages	45ml (3 tablespoons) soy sauce
3 cloves garlic	7.5ml (1½ teaspoons) rice wine
2 slices ginger	5ml (1 teaspoon) sugar
1 square red beancurd	salt to taste
7.5ml (1½ teaspoons) cornflour	oil for deep frying

Soak dried cabbage in water overnight. Rinse clean and chop finely. Trim bottoms from Chinese white cabbages; discard old leaves. Finely chop garlic and ginger. Mash red beancurd. Mix cornflour with 15ml (1 tablespoon) water.

Simmer the pork in boiling water for 40 minutes. Pat dry and paint with 15ml (1 tablespoon) soy sauce. Heat deep fat and fry pork for 2 minutes. Remove and cool before cutting into ½cm (¼-inch) slices. Arrange in a bowl. Mix the preserved cabbage with 15ml (1 tablespoon) soy sauce, the rice wine, garlic, ginger and beancurd, and put on top of the pork slices. Steam for 1 hour. Blanch the white cabbages, drain and arrange on the serving plate. Strain off the cooking juices from the pork, and put the pork on the plate. Heat the cooking liquor with 45ml (3 tablespoons) water, 15ml (1 tablespoon) soy sauce, the sugar and cornflour paste. Bring to the boil. Adjust the seasoning and pour over the pork. Serve.

Cantonese Sweet and Sour Pork

蜜汁咕嚕肉

400g (14 oz) lean pork steak	1 tomato
2 egg whites	60ml (4 tablespoons) sugar
5ml (1 teaspoon) salt	60ml (4 tablespoons) rice
15ml (1 tablespoon) rice wine	vinegar
75ml (5 tablespoons) cornflour	10ml (2 teaspoons) soy sauce
1 green pepper	20ml (4 teaspoons) tomato
50g (2 oz) fresh or canned	paste
pineapple	oil for deep frying
2 spring onions	2ml (½ teaspoon) sesame oil

Cut pork into 2cm (1-inch) cubes. Marinate with egg whites, salt, rice wine, and 30ml (2 tablespoons) cornflour for 15 minutes. Coat each cube in dry cornflour. Cut the green pepper, pineapple and spring onion into 2cm (1-inch) pieces. Peel and chop the tomato. Mix the sauce with sugar, vinegar, soy sauce, tomato paste, 60ml (4 tablespoons) water and 10ml (2 teaspoons) cornflour.

Heat oil in a pan and deep-fry the coated pork pieces over a high heat for 3 minutes. Remove and drain. Re-heat oil and fry pork again for 1-2 minutes. Drain well. Heat 30ml (2 tablespoons) oil in a pan and stir-fry the onion, pepper and pineapple. Pour in the sauce and bring to the boil. Add the pork and serve sprinkled with sesame oil.

43

Stewed Pork and Ham

火腿大白蹄

250g (8 oz) ham, as a piece
1kg (2 lb) pork leg (with skin)
2 white cabbages
75g (3 oz) bamboo shoots
2 spring onions
4 slices ginger
30ml (2 tablespoons) rice wine
10ml (2 teaspoons) salt

Wash ham. Wash pork leg clean; scrape hairs off skin. Push the lean meat back into the skin; then tie with string to keep it tight. Trim cabbages, cut lengthways in half. Open cabbage leaves gently to wash them clean. Slice bamboo shoots. Cut spring onions into sections.

Put ham in a casserole with water 3 times its volume; bring ham, rice wine, salt, spring onions and ginger to the boil. Remove yellow foam from surface. Keep boiling. Then add in pork leg. Add water to cover the leg. Remove foam after boiling. Lower heat and simmer for 45 minutes. Remove ham. Add in bamboo shoots, more water, and salt. Continue cooking for another 30 minutes. Test by sticking a fork in the pork: if the fork comes out easily, it is done. Add cabbages to the pot; boil till soft and remove. Place bamboo shoots and cabbage on soup plate. Cut off string on leg; put leg in middle of plate with sliced ham round it.

44

Steamed Lotus-leaf Packets

荷葉
䊦蒸肉

600g (1 lb 5 oz) belly of pork
60ml (4 tablespoons) soy sauce
10ml (2 teaspoons) salt
45ml (3 tablespoons) rice wine
4 dry lotus leaves
200g (7 oz) sweet potato
125g (4 oz) rice flour
10ml (2 teaspoons) wuxiang

Slice pork into 12 large, thin pieces. Marinate with soy sauce, salt and rice wine for 3 hours. Remove stems from lotus leaves; wash and cut each into 4-5 slices. Boil in water to soften for use as wrapping. Peel sweet potato; wash and chop into thin pieces. Mix rice flour and *wuxiang*. Lay a piece of wet cloth on a steamer. Spread sweet potato on the cloth evenly; sprinkle salt on top. Coat each slice of pork with the prepared rice flour; then wrap with one sheet of lotus leaf. Tie each packet with string; place all the packets in a steamer.

Steam pork and sweet potato over full heat for about 2 hours. Add water in pot to keep it boiling. When done, place a bed of sweet potato on a plate with the lotus-leaf packets on top. Serve.

45

Stir-fried Pork Shreds with Watercress

西洋菜炒肉丝

200g (7 oz) lean pork
2ml (½ teaspoon) salt
7.5ml (1½ teaspoons) rice wine
7.5ml (1½ teaspoons) cornflour
3 bunches watercress
1 spring onion
30ml (2 tablespoons) oil
10ml (2 teaspoons) soy sauce

Shred the pork and marinate with the salt, rice wine and conflour. Remove the old stems and leaves from the watercress. Wash and cut into 5cm (2-inch) lengths. Cut the spring onions into 1cm (½-inch) lengths.

Heat the oil and stir-fry the spring onion; then add the pork shreds. Stir-fry for 2 minutes, then put in the soy sauce and watercress. Stir-fry for another 2 minutes. Adjust the seasoning with salt and serve.

Note: beef may be substituted for pork, and celery for watercress.

Spiced Eight-jewels

八寶辣醬

200g (7 oz) belly of pork
3 squares beancurd
50g (2 oz) canned baby corn
50g (2 oz) bamboo shoots
50g (2 oz) water chestnuts
25g (1 oz) peanuts
2 spring onions
4 slices ginger
15ml (1 tablespoon) rice wine
50g (2 oz) cooked prawns
25g (1 oz) peas
10ml (2 teaspoons) chilli-bean sauce
10ml (2 teaspoons) soy sauce
sugar, salt and pepper
oil for deep frying

Cut pork into 2cm (1-inch) slices. Cut beancurd into 2cm (1-inch) cubes. Dice baby corn and bamboo shoots. Skin peanuts and deep-fry in moderately hot oil until golden. Drain. Cut 1 spring onion into sections.

Put pork slices into a pan with 2 slices ginger, 1 whole spring onion, the rice wine and 500ml (1 pint) water. Simmer for 20 minutes, then lift out and reserve stock. Heat 45ml (3 tablespoons) oil in a pan and stir-fry the remaining onion and ginger. Add the pork, then the vegetables and prawns. Pour in the reserved stock, chilli-bean sauce and soy sauce and bring to the boil. Slide in the beancurd and simmer for 5 minutes. Adjust the seasoning with salt, sugar and pepper and mix in the peanuts before serving.

Pork Chops in Sweet Bean Sauce

醬爆回鍋肉

500g (1 lb) pork from leg
15ml (1 tablespoon) rice wine
5ml (1 teaspoon) salt
1 spring onion
2 slices ginger
300g (10 oz) snow peas
2 chillis
15ml (1 tablespoon) sugar
45ml (3 tablespoons) sweet
    bean sauce

Marinate pork in rice wine, salt, spring onion and ginger.
Wash and trim snow peas. De-seed chillis, then slice at an
angle. Mix sugar and sweet bean sauce. If too dry, add some
water; mix well.

Steam pork till done. Slice thickly when cold. Heat 30ml
(2 tablespoons) oil over full heat, then lower the flame;
stir-fry chillis; add sweet paste; stir quickly, then remove.
Heat oil again; fry pork slices for 2 minutes, then peas and a
dash of salt; stir-fry quickly. Add the pork and sweet paste;
stir well till ready to serve.

Note: large spring onions can be used instead of snow peas.

Sweet and Sour Spareribs

糖醋小排骨

600g (1 lb 5 oz) pork spareribs
45ml (3 tablespoons) rice
    vinegar
90ml (6 tablespoons) soy sauce
30ml (2 tablespoons) rice wine
2 spring onions
45ml (3 tablespoons) cornflour
2 slices ginger
25ml (1½ tablespoons) sugar
oil for deep frying

Cut spareribs into 5cm (2-inch) sections. Marinate with 30ml
(2 tablespoons) vinegar, 45ml (3 tablespoons) soy sauce,
and 30ml (2 tablespoons) rice wine for 2 hours. Wash spring
onions. Mix 15ml (1 tablespoon) cornflour with 25ml (1½
tablespoons) water.

Heat the oil; quickly stir-fry the ginger and spring onions,
then add the pork ribs and fry until brown. Remove and
allow to cool. Sprinkle 30ml (2 tablespoons) cornflour on
the ribs; mix well. Re-heat oil and fry ribs again. Drain well.
Clean the pan; heat 30ml (2 tablespoons) oil over low heat;
add 15ml (1 tablespoon) vinegar, 25ml (1½ tablespoons)
sugar, 45ml (3 tablespoons) soy sauce, and 60ml (4
tablespoons) water. Bring to boil. Add the cornflour paste
and simmer until thickened. Put ribs in and mix well. Serve.

Pork and White Radish Pot

連鍋湯

500g (1 lb) pork, from leg
600g (1 lb 5 oz) white radish
2 spring onions
15ml (1 tablespoon) oil
3 slices ginger
400ml (⅔ pint, 2 cups) stock
7.5ml (1½ teaspoons) rice wine
5ml (1 teaspoon) ground Sichuan pepper
5ml (1 teaspoon) salt
7.5ml (1½ teaspoons) soy sauce

Scald the pork in boiling water. Let it cool down; slice as thinly as possible. Peel the white radish and slice 2-3cm (1-1½ inches) thick. Cut the spring onions into sections.

Heat the oil in a saucepan; stir-fry the spring onions and ginger. Add the white radish and stock. Bring to the boil and boil for 40 minutes. Then add the pork, rice wine, Sichuan pepper, salt and soy sauce. Cover. Simmer for about ½ hour. Serve.

50

Stuffed Beancurd with Beancurd Packets

麵麭百葉包肉

300g (10 oz) pork, from leg
5ml (1 teaspoon) salt
15ml (1 tablespoon) rice wine
15ml (1 tablespoon) cornflour
6 sheets dried beancurd
12 fried beancurd squares
50g (2 oz) silk noodles
50g (2 oz) spinach
15ml (1 tablespoon) soy sauce

Mince the pork and mix it with 2ml (½ teaspoon) salt, rice wine and cornflour. Soak the beancurd sheets for 5 minutes in hot water to soften. Pat dry and cut into 12 strips. Wrap a finger-sized roll of minced pork in each strip. Tie each roll with string. Steam for 40 minutes. Open a small hole on top of each fried beancurd; stuff with 2ml (½ teaspoon) mixed pork. Make 12 stuffed beancurd squares. Cut the noodles in half. Wash and trim the spinach. Blanch in boiling water, then refresh in cold water and drain.

Bring the beancurd rolls, 800ml (1⅓ pints, 4 cups) water and salt to the boil for a few minutes. Put in the stuffed beancurds; bring to the boil again. Then add the noodles and return to the boil. Add the soy sauce. Pour the soup into a large soup bowl. Untie the beancurd rolls and arrange them in the centre with the spinach. Serve.

Ants Climbing the Trees

肉末炸粉絲

200g (7 oz) minced pork
5ml (1 teaspoon) salt
15ml (1 tablespoon) rice wine
15ml (1 tablespoon) soy sauce
1 Chinese sausage
2 spring onions
2 chillis
50g (2 oz) silk noodles
oil for deep frying

Marinate the pork with salt, rice wine and soy sauce. Dice the sausage and mix with the pork. Add 30ml (2 tablespoons) water and mix well. Shred the spring onions and dice the chillis. Cut the noodles in half.

Heat 45ml (3 tablespoons) oil in a pan over full heat. Quickly stir-fry the minced pork until it is cooked. Add the chillis and spring onions; mix well and remove. Heat the deep fat and deep-fry the noodles until puffed and almost transparent. Press the noodles flat on a plate and spoon the pork over them. Serve.

Fried Pork Chops

炸裡肌肉

500g (1 lb) pork fillet
5ml (1 teaspoon) salt
25ml (1½ tablespoons) rice wine
25ml (1½ tablespoons) soy sauce
75g (3 oz) flour
75g (3 oz) fine breadcrumbs
2 eggs
1 potato
2 spring onions
2 slices ginger
oil for deep frying

Slice pork 5-6cm (2-2½ inches) thick. Pat with flat side of chopper to tenderize. Marinate with salt, rice wine and soy sauce. Let stand for 1 hour. Mix flour and breadcrumbs. Beat eggs well. Peel potato and slice thinly.

Heat the deep fat and fry the potato slices till golden brown. Lift out and drain. Re-heat the oil, then lower the flame. Deep-fry the spring onions and ginger first. Dip the pork slices in egg, then coat with flour. Fry in oil till brown. Do these a few pieces at a time. Drain well and arrange with the potato slices on a plate and serve.

Ham and Corn Soup

火肩双玉羹

1 can baby corn
1 can creamed corn
50g (2 oz) cooked ham or 1 Chinese sausage
75g (3 oz) pork
5ml (1 teaspoon) salt
5ml (1 teaspoon) rice wine
5ml (1 teaspoon) soy sauce
30ml (2 tablespoons) cornflour
2 spring onions
45ml (3 tablespoons) oil

Drain and slice baby corn into 1cm (½-inch)-thick sections. Shred ham or sausage. Mince pork and marinate with salt, rice wine, soy sauce and 5ml (1 teaspoon) cornflour. Cut off the green leaves from the spring onions. Chop the white. Mix remaining cornflour with 30ml (2 tablespoons) water.

Heat the oil in a pan; stir-fry the spring onion leaves, then add the minced pork. Keep stirring until the pork shreds separate. Pick out the onion leaves. Add the can of creamed corn and the baby corn shoots. Mix in 600ml (1 pint, 3 cups) water and the salt and bring to the boil. Then stir in the cornflour paste to make a thick soup. Sprinkle the chopped spring onion on top. Pour into a large soup bowl. Before serving spread ham shreds on top of the soup.

Note: this is a tasty (and pretty) dish which may also be served as a dessert.

Stir-fried Pork Kidneys with Cashew Nuts

火腿双腰

2 pork kidneys
5ml (1 teaspoon) salt
7.5ml (1½ teaspoons) rice wine
15ml (1 tablespoon) cornflour
½ cauliflower
1 spring onion
50g (2 oz) cashew nuts
7.5ml (1½ teaspoons) soy sauce
100g (4 oz) Parma ham, sliced
2 slices ginger
oil for deep frying

Cut open each kidney; remove the white core and fat in the centre. Lightly score the outside surface to make a criss-cross pattern. Then cut into small pieces. Rinse in water and pat dry. Marinate with salt, rice wine, and 7.5ml (1½ teaspoons) cornflour before cooking. Wash cauliflower clean. Tear into pieces. Cut spring onion into sections. Mix 7.5ml (1½ teaspoons) cornflour with 15ml (1 tablespoon) water.

Heat the deep fat, and fry cashew nuts over a low heat. Stir constantly until light brown, remove and drain. Heat 30ml (2 tablespoons) oil in a pan and stir-fry the cauliflower with a little salt. Add soy sauce and ham slices. Tip in 150ml (¼ pint, ½ cup) water and boil until cauliflower is cooked. Drain and reserve liquid. Heat 45ml (3 tablespoons) oil and stir-fry spring onion and ginger; add kidneys and cook for 1 minute. Return cauliflower and cashew nuts to pan with cooking liquor. Thicken with cornflour paste. Bring to the boil and serve.

Feather-duster Spareribs

拂手排骨

12 pork ribs (each 5-10cm/2-4 inches long)
30ml (2 tablespoons) cornflour
30ml (2 tablespoons) soy sauce
30ml (2 tablespoons) rice wine
pinch of salt
50g (2 oz) fresh or canned pineapple
50g (2 oz) carrot
50g (2 oz) onion
2 spring onions
30ml (2 tablespoons) rice vinegar
30ml (2 tablespoons) sugar
15ml (1 tablespoon) tomato paste
oil for deep frying

Marinate pork ribs with 15ml (1 tablespoon) each of cornflour, soy sauce, rice wine and a dash of salt; let stand for ½ hour. Cube pineapple and carrot. Shred onion and dice spring onions. Make cornflour paste with the remaining cornflour.

Heat oil in a pan, then add the ribs. Deep-fry over a moderate heat until golden brown. Lift out, drain and place the ribs on a plate. Heat 30ml (2 tablespoons) oil in a clean pan over a high heat. Stir-fry carrot, onion and pineapple. Add 15ml (1 tablespoon) soy sauce, the vinegar, sugar, tomato paste and 60ml (4 tablespoons) water; bring to the boil. Add cornflour paste to thicken. Pour over the ribs and serve.

Dungbo Pork

東坡四喜肉

750g (1½ lb) belly of pork (with skin)
300g (10 oz) spinach
2 spring onions
2 slices ginger
60ml (4 tablespoons) dark soy sauce
25g (1 oz) crystal sugar
15ml (1 tablespoon) rice wine
5ml (1 teaspoon) salt
30ml (2 tablespoons) oil

Clean pork skin by pulling hairs off with tweezers and scrape till really clean. Wash spinach clean. Remove tough ribs. Cook spinach in boiling water. Rinse and drain.

Blanch the pork in boiling water. Rinse and drain. Heat 15ml (1 tablespoon) oil in a pan; add the sugar and soy sauce; stir constantly over low heat until sugar melts. Add the pork; stir so that the sauce coats the pork evenly. Add the spring onions, ginger, rice wine and sufficient water to cover at least half the pork. Stew the pork, skin-side down, until very tender and loose. During stewing, keep moving the pork to avoid it being burnt at the bottom. If necessary add more water. When done, pick out the ginger and spring onions. Remove pork. Score a deep cross on the pork to make it look like 4 pieces of meat. Put the pork on to a dish with the spinach and pour over the remaining sauce. Serve.

Note: this dish is called after Su Dungbo, a literary figure of the Song Dynasty.

59

Deep-fried Pork with Arrowheads

菱角走油肉

400g (14 oz) belly pork (with skin)
2 spring onions
2 slices ginger
15ml (1 tablespoon) rice wine
75ml (5 tablespoons) soy sauce
25g (1 oz) crystal sugar
5ml (1 teaspoon) salt
200g (7 oz) canned arrowheads
oil for deep frying

Clean pork skin. Put the pork, spring onions, ginger and rice wine into a pan with sufficient water to cover and bring to the boil. Skim off the foam. Lower heat and simmer until the pork is tender, adding more water when necessary. Turn the pork from time to time. Lift out and drain; reserve the cooking liquor. Heat the deep fat, then over a moderate heat slide in the pork, skin-side down. Take care, for the oil will spit. Cover the pan and deep-fry the pork until the skin is brown, turning it over in the oil if possible. Remove and drain. Re-heat the oil and return the pork to the pan. Fry over a low heat until the skin is dark brown and blistering. Remove and drain. Put the soy sauce, sugar and salt into a pan with the reserved cooking liquor together with the pork. Add enough water to cover. Simmer for 45 minutes, turning the pork in the liquid. Lift out and slice thinly. Drop the arrowheads into the cooking liquor and boil for 3 minutes. Lift out and drain. Arrange arrowheads on a plate with the pork slices on top. Serve.

Bacon Soup

燉
醃鲜肉湯

600g (1¼ lb) bacon
400g (15 oz) pork
300g (10 oz) bamboo shoots
6 sticks dried beancurd
2 spring onions
5ml (1 teaspoon) salt
15ml (1 tablespoon) rice wine
2 slices ginger

Rinse bacon in hot water, then cold water. Cut pork into 2-3cm (1-1½-inch) cubes. Cut the bamboo shoots into wedge-shaped pieces. Soak the beancurd sticks overnight and then cut into 5cm (2-inch) lengths.

Put the bacon into a pan of water. The amount of water used should be 2-3 times the volume of the bacon. Add the rice wine, a dash of salt, spring onions and ginger. Bring to the boil. Remove the foam from the surface. Keep boiling. Add the pork. When boiling again, skim off the foam. When the bacon is tender, remove. Add more water if necessary. Put in the bamboo shoots and boil for 5 minutes, then add the beancurd sticks and boil for another 3 minutes. Adjust the seasoning to taste with salt and serve in a large soup bowl with the bacon sliced on top.

61

Red-cooked Pork Hocks

五香
猪爪

3 pork hocks
3 spring onions
3 slices ginger
15ml (1 tablespoon) rice wine
45ml (3 tablespoons) soy sauce
1ml (¼ teaspoon) wuxiang
2ml (½ teaspoon) salt
12g (½ oz) crystal sugar
spinach leaves for garnish

Ask your butcher to cut the hocks into 8cm (3-inch) sections. Blanch the pork hocks in boiling water and then rinse. Put them with the spring onions, ginger, rice wine, soy sauce, *wuxiang* and salt into a pan and cover with water. Bring to the boil, cover the pan and simmer over a low heat for 3 hours. Add more water if necessary and turn the hock pieces in the sauce. Add the sugar and cook for another 30 minutes until the sauce is much reduced. Serve garnished with blanched spinach leaves.
Note: this is a good dish to serve with noodles.

Stir-fried Meatballs

梅花大團圓

500g (1 lb) minced pork
6 water chestnuts
5ml (1 teaspoon) salt
15ml (1 tablespoon) rice wine
30ml (2 tablespoons) soy sauce
15ml (1 tablespoon) cornflour
6 small green peppers
2 slices ginger
oil for deep frying

Dice the water chestnuts and mix with the minced pork, salt, rice wine, 15ml (1 tablespoon) soy sauce and the cornflour. Divide into five and shape into balls between your hands. (It is easier to do this if your hands are wet.)

De-seed and cut each pepper in half.

Heat the deep fat and deep-fry the green pepper halves for 30 seconds. Do not let them brown. Lift out and drain. Heat 45ml (3 tablespoons) oil in a pan and stir-fry the ginger. Add the meatballs and brown on both sides. Add the remaining soy sauce and 275ml (½ pint, 1¼ cups) of water and simmer until the pan is almost dry. Remove the meatballs and arrange them in the centre of a plate with the 12 pepper halves around them. Serve.

Pork with Red Beancurd Sauce

腐乳滷肉

850g (1¾ lb) pork belly with skin
2 red beancurd squares
45ml (3 tablespoons) red beancurd juice
30ml (2 tablespoons) crystal sugar
4 spring onions
2 slices ginger
30ml (2 tablespoons) rice wine
15ml (1 tablespoon) oil
salt
strips of spring onion

Carefully strip the hairs from the pork skin and rinse clean. Mash the fermented beancurd. Mix the mash with 30ml (3 tablespoons) water and its juice. If necessary crush the sugar. Dice the spring onions.

Heat 15ml (1 tablespoon) oil in a pan over a low heat and stir-fry half the spring onions. Add the beancurd sauce and the sugar. Stir constantly until the sugar is melted. Remove. Put the pork in a pan, skin-side-down, with sufficient water to cover. Add the remaining spring onion, ginger and rice wine. Remove foam from the surface, then simmer the meat for 2 hours. Keep turning it during the cooking. Then add a little more water and a pinch of salt, and pour the beancurd sauce over the meat. Bring to the boil and cook for another 30 minutes, basting the meat frequently with the sauce. Serve garnished with spring onion strips and with the remaining sauce poured over.

Steamed Sweet Ham with Bread

富貴
火腿

600g (1¼ lb) ham, boned, as a piece
380g (13 oz) crystal sugar
1 small white loaf

1 cook-in bag
string

Soak the ham for 6 hours, then cut into slices 2 x 3cm (1 x 1½ inches) and ½cm (¼ inch) thick. Place in the bag and sprinkle 110g (4 oz) sugar over the ham. Tie into a tidy rectangular shape. Steam the ham packet for about 2 hours over a low heat. It will turn red and slightly sticky. Melt the remaining sugar in a pan to make a syrup. Untie the packet and discard the gravy. Arrange the ham slices on a plate and pour over the syrup. Trim the crust from the bread and slice so that every two slices are joined at one end, to make a V-shape. Steam until soft.

Each person puts a slice of ham into a double slice of bread and holds it in their hand to eat.

65

Sweet Dates and Ham

600g (1¼ lb) cooked ham
14 black or red dates
100ml (4 fl oz, ½ cup) water
30ml (2 tablespoons) honey

Skin the ham and remove fat; slice thinly. Wash dates clean and soak for 3 hours.

Place the ham slices on one side of a plate with the dates on the other. Steam until the ham is tender (about 30 minutes). Discard the juice. Transfer the ham and dates to another plate. Boil the honey and water to make a thick syrup. Pour over the ham and serve.

Steamed Pearl Balls

珍珠
肉圆

75g (3 oz) glutinous rice
5 water chestnuts
450g (1 lb) minced pork
5ml (1 teaspoon) salt
7.5ml (1½ teaspoons) rice wine
30ml (2 tablespoons) soy sauce
15ml (1 tablespoon) cornflour
watercress and chilli for garnish

Wash the rice and soak it in water for 4-5 hours. Drain. Dice the water chestnuts. Marinate the minced pork with the diced water chestnuts. Add salt, rice wine, soy sauce and cornflour. Stir well and shape into balls about 4cm (1½ inches) across. Roll the balls in glutinous rice to coat evenly.

Steam the rice-coated meatballs for 45 minutes over medium heat. Add more water in if there is not enough in the steamer. Arrange on a plate and garnish with blanched watercress and threads of chilli. Serve.

69

Dry-fried Beef Shreds

乾燒牛肉絲

600g (1¼ lb) beef steak
30ml (2 tablespoons) rice wine
5ml (1 teaspoon) salt
5ml (1 teaspoon) sugar
100g (4 oz) carrot
250g (8 oz) celery
2 spring onions
2 slices ginger

15ml (1 tablespoon) chilli-bean sauce
5ml (1 teaspoon) ground Sichuan pepper
15ml (1 tablespoon) rice vinegar
5ml (1 teaspoon) sesame oil
oil for deep frying

Shred the beef and marinate with 15ml (1 tablespoon) rice wine, 2ml (½ teaspoon) salt and the sugar. Peel and shred the carrot. Wash and cut the celery into 4cm (1½-inch) lengths. Cut the spring onions into 1cm (½-inch) lengths.

Deep-fry the beef shreds in hot oil for 4 minutes, then lift out and drain. Heat 30ml (2 tablespoons) oil and stir-fry the onion and ginger. Add the chilli-bean sauce, then the carrot. After 30 seconds add the celery and 3ml (½ teaspoon) salt and cook until the carrot is soft. Then add 15ml (1 tablespoon) rice wine, the Sichuan pepper and vinegar. Mix in the beef, sprinkle with sesame oil and serve.

'Fish-fragrant' Beef

魚香牛腩

600g (1¼ lb) topside of beef, as a piece
45ml (3 tablespoons) soy sauce
30ml (2 tablespoons) rice wine
4 spring onions
2 slices ginger
5ml (1 teaspoon) grated ginger
2 cloves garlic, crushed
5ml (1 teaspoon) chilli powder (optional)

15ml (1 tablespoon) chilli-bean sauce
15ml (1 tablespoon) sesame oil
5ml (1 teaspoon) red vinegar
15ml (1 tablespoon) sugar
10ml (2 teaspoons) cornflour
15ml (1 tablespoon) oil

Put the beef into a pan with 30ml (2 tablespoons) soy sauce, 15ml (1 tablespoon) rice wine, 2 onions and 2 slices ginger and cover with water. Boil for 1 hour; reserve the cooking liquor. Finely chop 2 spring onions and mix with the remaining ingredients except the oil to make a 'fish-fragrant' sauce.

Slice the beef into ½cm (¼-inch)-thick slices and arrange on a plate with the reserved liquor. Steam for 20 minutes, then drain off the liquid and reserve again. Heat 15ml (1 tablespoon) oil and pour in the 'fish-fragrant' sauce and the reserved cooking stock. Bring to the boil and pour over the beef. Serve.

71

Mongolian Fire-pot

涮羊肉

1kg (2 lb) thinly sliced lean lamb
250g (8 oz) thinly sliced lambs' liver
500g (1 lb) Chinese cabbage
500g (1 lb) spinach
250g (8 oz) beancurd
180g (6 oz) silk noodles
1.2 litres (2 pints, 5 cups) well-seasoned
    boiling stock

Ingredients for dipping sauces:
soy sauce, sesame oil, sesame paste, sweet
bean sauce, red beancurd juice, chilli oil,
chilli-bean sauce, rice wine, rice vinegar,
sugar, coriander and spring onion

Arrange the sliced meats on several plates. Wash the Chinese cabbage and spinach and cut into small pieces. Cut the silk noodles into short lengths and soak in warm water for 5 minutes. Cut the beancurd into thick slices. Arrange on several plates. Chop the coriander and spring onions.

Pour the boiling stock into the fire-pot and take to the table. Allow to return to full boil. Arrange all the plates of ingredients around the pot.

Each diner mixes his own dipping sauce in his bowl.

Then, each diner holds a piece of meat in the boiling stock with his chopsticks until it is cooked, then dips it in his sauce before eating.

After the meat is finished put the beancurd, silk noodles and vegetables into the stock. Simmer for 2 minutes and serve as soup.

Note: charcoal-burning fire-pots should only be used in well-ventilated rooms.

Beef with Choisam and Oyster Sauce

蠔油牛肉

300g (10 oz) beef steak
10ml (2 teaspoons) soy sauce
7.5ml (1½ teaspoons) sugar
10ml (2 teaspoons) cornflour
300g (10 oz) choisam
2 spring onions
2 slices ginger
30ml (2 tablespoons) oyster sauce
30ml (2 tablespoons) rice wine
2ml (½ teaspoon) salt
oil for deep frying

Slice the beef thinly and marinate with the soy sauce, 2ml (½ teaspoon) sugar and 5ml (1 teaspoon) cornflour. Wash and cut the *choisam* into 5cm (2-inch) lengths. Cut the spring onions into 1cm (½-inch) lengths. Mix 5ml (1 teaspoon) cornflour with 75ml (5 tablespoons, ¼ cup) water.

Heat the oil and deep-fry the beef slices for 30 seconds. Drain well. Heat 45ml (3 tablespoons) oil in a pan and stir-fry the *choisam* with 15ml (1 tablespoon) rice wine and the salt for 3 minutes. Drain and arrange on the serving plate. Re-heat pan with 15ml (1 tablespoon) oil. Stir-fry the onions and ginger, add the beef, then the oyster sauce, 5ml (1 teaspoon) sugar, rice wine and cornflour paste. Bring to the boil and spoon over the *choisam*. Serve.

Braised Beef

貴妃牛肉

400g (14 oz) braising steak
150g (5 oz) carrots
5 spring onions
2 cloves garlic
15ml (1 tablespoon) cornflour
30ml (2 tablespoons) oil
5ml (1 teaspoon) chilli oil
2 slices ginger
600ml (1 pint, 2½ cups) good stock
15ml (1 tablespoon) soy sauce
30ml (2 tablespoons) tomato paste
15ml (1 tablespoon) sugar
10ml (2 teaspoons) rice vinegar
30ml (2 tablespoons) rice wine

Trim and cut the beef into thick slices. Peel and dice the carrots. Cut the spring onions into 5cm (2-inch) lengths and slice the garlic. Mix the cornflour with 30ml (2 tablespoons) water.

Dip the beef slices in boiling water for 2 minutes. Then rinse and drain. Heat the oil and stir-fry the carrot for 2 minutes, then lift out. Add the chilli oil to the pan and stir-fry the onion, ginger and garlic. Stir in the rest of the ingredients. Return the beef and carrots to the pan; cover and simmer over a low heat for 1 hour. Thicken with the cornflour paste and adjust the seasoning before serving.

Spiced Beef Pot

红烧
牛腩煲

600g (1¼ lb) beef shin
4 spring onions
12g (½ oz) ginger as a piece
4 cloves garlic
15ml (1 tablespoon) oil
75ml (5 tablespoons) soy sauce
15ml (1 tablespoon) rice wine
25g (1 oz) crystal sugar
15g (½ oz) total weight of Sichuan
    peppercorns, star anise, cinnamon,
    cloves, fennel, dried orange peel, tied
    in a small bag
coriander leaves

Cut the beef into 4cm (1½-inch) cubes. Cut the spring onions into 5cm (2-inch) lengths and crush the ginger. Chop the garlic.

Heat the oil in a pan and stir-fry the garlic over a high heat. Add the beef and stir-fry for another 2 minutes. Then put in the ginger, spring onions, soy sauce, rice wine and 1.4 litres (2¼ pints, 5½ cups) water. Add the spice bag and sugar and bring to the boil. Transfer to a casserole, cover tightly and cook for 3 hours over a low heat. Remove the spice bag, adjust the seasoning and garnish with coriander. Serve.

Beef Shreds with Asparagus

150g (5 oz) beef steak
5ml (1 teaspoon) salt
7.5ml (1½ teaspoons) rice wine
7.5ml (1½ teaspoons) cornflour
275g (9 oz) asparagus
2 chillis
2 spring onions
2 slices ginger
15ml (1 tablespoon) soy sauce
oil for deep frying

Cut the beef into thin shreds and marinate with the salt, rice wine and cornflour for 30 minutes. Wash the asparagus, discard the tough stems and cut into 6cm (2½-inch) lengths. De-seed the chillis and cut slant-wise. Cut the spring onions into 1cm (½-inch) lengths.

Heat the oil and deep-fry the beef for 20 seconds. Drain well. Heat 30ml (2 tablespoons) oil in a pan and stir-fry the asparagus. After 30 seconds add a little salt and 150ml (¼ pint, ½ cup) water. Cook until just soft. Lift out and drain. Re-heat the pan with 30ml (2 tablespoons) oil and stir-fry the chillis, onion and ginger for 30 seconds. Add the beef, then the asparagus. Mix well, season with soy sauce and serve.

Braised Lamb with Red Dates

红枣羊肉

750g (1½ lb) lamb leg chops
12 red dates
250g (8 oz) white radish
3 spring onions
12g (½ oz) ginger, as a piece
12g (½ oz) crystal sugar
45ml (3 tablespoons) rice wine
5ml (1 teaspoon) salt
60ml (4 tablespoons) soy sauce

Remove the bones from the chops and cut into 5cm (2-inch) cubes. Soak the red dates in water for 3 hours. Peel and cut the white radish into wedges. Bruise the ginger and break the crystal sugar into small pieces.

Put the lamb into boiling water, return to the boil, then drain and rinse the meat well. Then put the lamb, red dates, ginger, onion, sugar, rice wine, salt and soy sauce into a pan with 900ml (1½ pints, 3½ cups) water and bring to the boil. Reduce the heat and simmer until the lamb is cooked (about 30 minutes). Take out the meat and red dates. Put the white radish into the stock with 275ml (½ pint, 1¼ cups) more water. Simmer for 50 minutes, then return the meat and dates to the pan for about 5 minutes. Adjust the seasoning and serve.

Chinese-style Beef Steak

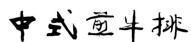

500g (1 lb) rump steak
15ml (1 tablespoon) lemon juice
1 egg yolk
20ml (4 teaspoons) cornflour
10ml (2 teaspoons) sugar
75g (3 oz) onion
30ml (2 tablespoons) soy sauce
30ml (2 tablespoons) tomato paste
10ml (2 teaspoons) chilli oil
15ml (1 tablespoon) water
10ml (2 teaspoons) vinegar
salt
oil for deep frying

Slice the beef into 1cm (½-inch)-thick slices. Pound with the blunt edge of a cleaver to tenderize, then marinate with the lemon juice, egg yolk, 15ml (1 tablespoon) cornflour, 5ml (1 teaspoon) sugar and 15ml (1 tablespoon) oil for 30 minutes. Then add 45ml (3 tablespoons) water to the marinade and mix well to coat the beef evenly.

Shred the onion. Mix the seasoning sauce of soy sauce, tomato paste, chilli oil, water, vinegar, 5ml (1 teaspoon) sugar and 5ml (1 teaspoon) cornflour.

Heat 15ml (1 tablespoon) oil in a pan and stir-fry the onion shreds for 1 minute. Pour in the seasoning sauce and bring to the boil. Adjust the seasoning with salt and keep warm beside the stove.

Heat the oil and deep-fry the beef for about 4 minutes. Then lift out, drain and arrange on a plate. Pour over the sauce and serve garnished with spring onion flowers and shreds of red cabbage.

Palace Beef

天厨牛肉

600g (1¼ lb) shin of beef, as a piece
30ml (2 tablespoons) ground Sichuan pepper
75ml (5 tablespoons) sea salt
5 spring onions
8 slices ginger
45ml (3 tablespoons) soy sauce
30ml (2 tablespoons) rice wine
15ml (1 tablespoon) crystal sugar

Rub the beef all over with 15ml (1 tablespoon) ground Sichuan pepper and the salt. Leave in the refrigerator for a week and then rinse well. Cut the spring onions into 5cm (2-inch) lengths.

Scald the beef in boiling water, then put it with the onions, ginger, soy sauce, rice wine and sugar into a pan with sufficient water to cover the meat. Cover the pan with a lid and simmer for 4 hours. Then remove the meat and leave to cool. When cold, cut into thin slices and arrange on a plate.

Chilli Breast of Lamb

1kg (2 lb) breast of lamb, including rib
   bones
500g (1 lb) Chinese white cabbage
6 spring onions
4 chillis
6 slices ginger
10ml (2 teaspoons) cornflour
15g (½ oz) sugar
15ml (1 tablespoon) soy sauce
15ml (1 tablespoon) black rice vinegar
15ml (1 tablespoon) rice wine
Optional additional seasoning:
  5ml (1 teaspoon) chilli powder
  5ml (1 teaspoon) finely chopped spring
    onion
  5ml (1 teaspoon) finely chopped ginger
  20ml (4 teaspoons) soy sauce
  15ml (1 tablespoon) chopped coriander
oil

Cut the breast into individual ribs.
Trim fat as desired. Wash and trim the
cabbages. Cut the spring onions into
1cm (½-inch) lengths and slice the
chillis. Mix the cornflour with 15ml (1
tablespoon) water.

Heat the oil and deep-fry the ribs
for 2 minutes. Lift out and drain. Heat
30ml (2 tablespoons) oil in a pan and
stir-fry the spring onions, chillis and
ginger. Add the sugar and cook over a
moderate heat until it has melted. Lift
from the fire and pour in the soy
sauce, black vinegar and rice wine.
Mix well and add 570ml (1 pint, 2½
cups) water. Put in the lamb and
simmer for 2 hours. Heat 15ml (1
tablespoon) oil and stir-fry the cabbage. Add a little water and cook until
soft. Drain and arrange on the serving
plate. Lay the lamb ribs on top. Heat
15ml (1 tablespoon) oil in a pan and
stir-fry the chilli powder, finely chopped spring onion and ginger. Pour in
the remaining cooking liquor from the
lamb. Adjust the seasoning with soy
and thicken with the cornflour paste.
Pour the thickened sauce over the
lamb and cabbage and serve sprinkled with chopped coriander.

Spiced Lamb Jelly

五香羊糕

600g (1¼ lb) leg of lamb, boned
250g (8 oz) white radish
5g (¼ oz) agar-agar
12g (½ oz) ginger, as a piece
2 spring onions
45ml (3 tablespoons) rice wine
1 star anise
45ml (3 tablespoons) soy sauce
salt
7.5ml (1½ teaspoons) shredded ginger
15ml (1 tablespoon) red vinegar

Cut the lamb into 5cm (2-inch) cubes. Peel the white radish and cut into two. Soak the *agar-agar* in hot water for 30 minutes. Drain. Crush the ginger.

Put the lamb, white radish and 15ml (1 tablespoon) rice wine in a pan with sufficient water to cover. Bring to a fast boil, then lift out the lamb. Discard the white radish and water. Put the lamb in a clean pan with the ginger, spring onions, star anise, soy sauce and 30ml (2 tablespoons) rice wine. Add sufficient water to cover and simmer until the lamb is tender (about 1 hour). Add the *agar-agar*, and more water if necessary, and continue cooking, stirring all the time until the water and meat are equal in quantity. Discard the onions, ginger and star anise. Adjust the flavour with salt. Tear the meat into shreds with two forks and put it with the remaining liquid into a square container to set. When cold, slice thickly and garnish with ginger shreds. Serve with a dipping sauce of red vinegar.

Chicken Shreds in Egg White

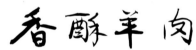

350g (12 oz) chicken breast
3 spring onions
5 slices ginger
5ml (1 teaspoon) Sichuan peppercorns
15ml (1 tablespoon) rice wine
5ml (1 teaspoon) salt
5 egg whites
15ml (1 tablespoon) cornflour
15ml (1 tablespoon) oil

Marinate the chicken with spring onion, ginger, Sichuan peppercorns, rice wine and salt for 30 minutes, then steam for 40 minutes. Beat the egg whites until stiff and fold in the cornflour.

Tear the chicken meat into shreds and pat dry. Divide the egg white in half and put one half on a plate. Sprinkle the chicken shreds over the egg and cover them with the remaining egg white. Heat a frying-pan with the oil and slide in the chicken and egg without disturbing the arrangement. Fry over a moderate heat, turning once. Serve cut into slices with Chinese pancakes (see page 114) and peppersalt dip.

Note: to make peppersalt: dry-fry 15ml (1 tablespoon) ground Sichuan pepper with 30ml (2 tablespoons) sea salt until it smells good, and serve as a dip.

Steamed Chicken and Scallop Balls

貝球鳳胆

300g (10 oz) chicken breast
30ml (2 tablespoons) rice wine
2ml (½ teaspoon) salt
2 large dried mushrooms
150g (5 oz) frozen scallops
3 egg whites
2 egg yolks
30ml (2 tablespoons) oil
25g (1 oz) cooked ham
150g (5 oz) spinach
60ml (4 tablespoons) chicken stock
5ml (1 teaspoon) cornflour

12 Chinese soup spoons

Cut the chicken into small pieces and put them with 15ml (1 tablespoon) rice wine and the salt into a food processor and work into a paste. Soak the mushrooms until soft. Discard the stalks and slice the caps thinly. De-frost the scallops and marinate in 15ml (1 tablespoon) rice wine for 20 minutes. Then steam for 10 minutes and cut into shreds. Beat the egg whites lightly and mix into the chicken paste. Beat the egg yolks. Heat 15ml (1 tablespoon) oil and make an omelette. Cut into thin strips. Cut the ham into thin strips.

Grease the spoons. Scoop up ½ spoonful of chicken paste. Then add a few scallop shreds and cover with more chicken paste. Smooth over with the back of a wet spoon and decorate with strips of egg, ham and mushroom. Use a separate spoon for each ball. Wash and trim the spinach. Mix the cornflour with 15ml (1 tablespoon) water.

Place the filled spoons in a steamer and steam for 35 minutes, then arrange on a plate. Stir-fry the spinach in 15ml (1 tablespoon) oil and a pinch of salt. Boil the stock and thicken with the cornflour. Pour over the spinach and chicken balls before serving.

Crystal Chicken Jelly

水晶凍鷄

600g (1¼ lb) chicken joints
10g (⅓ oz) agar-agar
5ml (1 teaspoon) salt
2 spring onions
4 slices ginger
45ml (3 tablespoons) rice wine
parsley leaves

Wash and dry the chicken. Soak the *agar-agar* in warm water for 30 minutes.

Put the chicken with the salt, spring onions, ginger, rice wine and 800ml (1½ pints, 3½ cups) water in a pan and bring to the boil. Skim well, then cover and boil gently for 45 minutes. Take out the chicken, strain and reserve the stock. Tear the chicken into shreds. Remove any fat from the stock and measure 570ml (1 pint, 2½ cups) into a pan. Bring to the boil, add the *agar-agar* and stir until dissolved. Put some parsley leaves in the bottom of a bowl, lay the chicken shreds on top and pour over the prepared stock. Refrigerate until set. Turn out and serve.

Steamed Ham with Pears

凉拌鷄肫肝

250g (8 oz) sweet-cured cooked
    ham
250g (8 oz) pears
45ml (3 tablespoons) oil
10ml (2 teaspoons) cornflour
50g (2 oz) crystal sugar
10ml (2 teaspoons) rice wine

Cut the ham into thin slices. Peel and cut the pears into bite-sized pieces. Heat the oil in a pan and stir-fry the pears to coat in the oil. Mix the cornflour with 15ml (1 tablespoon) water.

Arrange the ham slices round the sides of a bowl. Put the sugar in the middle and cover with the pears. Steam for 1 hour. Drain off the liquor and bring to the boil with the cornflour paste and rice wine. Turn out the ham so it lies on top of the pears and pour over the sauce before serving.

Steamed Chicken with Gingko Nuts and Red Dates

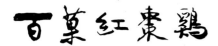

1.5kg (3 lb) chicken
14 red dates
1 spring onion
10ml (2 teaspoons) cornflour
7.5ml (1½ teaspoons) sugar
28 canned gingko nuts
2 slices ginger
5ml (1 teaspoon) Sichuan peppercorns
1 star anise
30ml (2 tablespoons) soy sauce
25ml (1½ tablespoons) rice wine
7.5ml (1½ teaspoons) salt
oil for deep frying

Chop the chicken into 6cm (2½-inch) pieces. Wash the red dates and soak in water for 2 hours. Cut the spring onions into 1cm (½-inch) lengths. Mix cornflour with 15ml (1 tablespoon) water.

Deep-fry the chicken pieces until browned, then lift out and drain. Put the red dates and sugar into 200ml (⅓ pint, ¾ cup) water and simmer until the syrup has almost gone. Tip out on to a large plate and mix with the gingko nuts. Heat 15ml (1 tablespoon) oil and stir-fry the onion, ginger, Sichuan pepper and star anise. Pour in the soy sauce, rice wine, salt and 275ml (½ pint, 1¼ cups) water. Add a pinch of sugar and the chicken. Mix well and simmer for 5 minutes, turning the chicken pieces in the sauce to ensure they are evenly coated. Pour the chicken and sauce over the gingko nuts and red dates and steam them all for 30 minutes over a high heat. Drain off the liquid into a pan and bring to the boil. Adjust the seasoning with salt and sugar and thicken with the cornflour paste. Pour over the chicken and serve.

Crispy Chicken with Peppersalt

椒盐香酥鸡

1.5kg (3 lb) chicken
30ml (2 tablespoons) salt
30ml (2 tablespoons) rice wine
2 spring onions
3 slices ginger
75g (3 oz) flour
30ml (2 tablespoons) fine breadcrumbs
1 egg
oil for deep frying
peppersalt (see page 84)

Chop the chicken in half lengthwise. Rub both inside and outside with the salt and rice wine. Cut the spring onions and chop the ginger slices. Scatter ginger and spring onions over the chicken and marinate for 1 hour. Mix together the flour and breadcrumbs. Make the peppersalt.

Steam the chicken for 30 minutes, then leave to cool. Discard the onion and ginger. Beat the egg and paint it all over the chicken. Roll the chicken halves in the flour mixture. Make sure they are well coated. Heat the deep fat and fry one half of the chicken at a time over a moderate heat until golden brown. Lift out and drain. Re-heat the oil and deep-fry each chicken half again over a high heat for about 2 minutes. Lift out and drain before arranging on a plate. Serve with a side dip of peppersalt.

Stir-fried Chicken with Walnuts

核桃鸡片

75g (3 oz) walnut halves
250g (8 oz) chicken breast
5ml (1 teaspoon) salt
7.5ml (1½ teaspoons) rice wine
7.5ml (1½ teaspoons) cornflour
1 green pepper
2 spring onions
3 slices ginger
15ml (1 tablespoon) soy sauce
15ml (1 tablespoon) tomato paste
10ml (2 teaspoons) rice vinegar
10ml (2 teaspoons) sugar
oil for deep frying

Soak the walnuts in hot water for 30 minutes, then rub off the skins. Thinly slice the chicken into small slices. Marinate with salt, rice wine, cornflour and 15ml (1 tablespoon) water. Mix well before cooking. De-seed the green pepper; cut into small pieces. Cut the spring onions into 1cm (½-inch) lengths.

Heat the oil, deep-fry the chicken slices for 30 seconds, then lift out and drain. Re-heat the oil and deep-fry the skinned walnuts over a moderate heat for 5 minutes. Drain well. Heat 30ml (2 tablespoons) oil in a pan and stir-fry the spring onion and ginger. Add the green pepper and stir-fry for 30 seconds before adding the chicken slices. Continue to stir-fry for another minute, then lift from the heat and mix in the soy sauce, tomato paste, rice vinegar, sugar and 15ml (1 tablespoon) water. Finally, bring to the boil, add the walnuts and serve.

90

Tossed Chicken and Beancurd Shreds

雞絲拌乾絲

2 squares beancurd
200g (7 oz) breast of chicken
1 carrot
2 spring onions
600ml (1 pint) chicken stock
2 slices ginger
45ml (3 tablespoons) rice wine
10ml (2 teaspoons) sesame oil

Press beancurd squares between two plates for 2 hours, then cut into thin strips. Shred the carrot. Cut the spring onion into 1cm (½-inch) lengths.

Bring the stock to the boil and add the onion, ginger and rice wine. Put in the chicken breast and simmer for 30 minutes. Lift out and drain before tearing into shreds. Put the carrot into the stock and boil for 2 minutes. Drain well. Leave the stock to cool and then mix 45ml (3 tablespoons) stock with the sesame oil. Arrange the strips of beancurd on a plate with the carrot and chicken. Pour over the stock and sesame sauce and serve.

Gungbao Chicken

宮保鷄丁

500g (1 lb) chicken
30ml (2 tablespoons) soy sauce
15ml (1 tablespoon) cornflour
15ml (1 tablespoon) rice wine
60g (2½ oz) peanuts
4 spring onions
8 dried red chillis
3 slices ginger
10ml (2 teaspoons) sugar
salt
10ml (2 teaspoons) sesame oil
oil for deep frying

Dice the chicken; marinate for 30 minutes in 15ml (1 tablespoon) soy sauce and the cornflour and rice wine. Skin the peanuts by dipping them in boiling water. Cut the spring onions into 2cm (1-inch) lengths and the chillis in halves.

Heat the oil and deep-fry chicken dice for 2 minutes. Drain well. Re-heat oil and fry peanuts for 3 minutes. Drain. Heat a pan with 45ml (3 tablespoons) oil and stir-fry ginger, spring onions and chillis. Add chicken dice and stir-fry for another minute before stirring in 15ml (1 tablespoon) soy sauce and the sugar. Adjust seasoning with salt and mix in the peanuts. Serve sprinkled with sesame oil.

Strange-flavoured Chicken

1kg (2 lb) cold chicken
15ml (1 tablespoon) finely diced
   spring onion
15ml (1 tablespoon) finely
   chopped ginger
7.5ml (1½ teaspoons) crushed
   garlic
7.5ml (1½ teaspoons) sugar
30ml (2 tablespoons) sesame
   paste
30ml (2 tablespoons) soy sauce
15ml (1 tablespoon) rice
   vinegar
15ml (1 tablespoon) sesame oil
10ml (2 teaspoons) chilli oil
5ml (1 teaspoon) salt
5ml (1 teaspoon) ground
   Sichuan pepper

Tear the chicken into shreds. Mix all the other ingredients into a sauce.

Put the chicken shreds on a plate and pour over the seasoning sauce. Mix well and serve garnished with lettuce leaves.

Plum Blossom Pigeons

五梅雛鴿

5 pigeons
100g (4 oz) glutinous rice
20 red dates
3 dried mushrooms
60g (2½ oz) minced pork
600ml (1 pint) stock
2 spring onions
2 slices ginger
2ml (1½ teaspoon) Sichuan peppercorns
2 petals star anise
15ml (1 tablespoon) rice wine
2ml (½ teaspoon) salt
15ml (1 tablespoon) soy sauce
5ml (1 teaspoon) sugar
Optional garnish: carved dyed white radish

Split the pigeons through the backbones to open them out. Rinse well. Wash the glutinous rice in several lots of water, soak for 30 minutes then drain. Soak the red dates for 3 hours. Remove stones and chop. Soak the mushrooms in warm water for 30 minutes. Discard stalks and chop caps finely.

Put the pigeons, stock, spring onions, ginger, Sichuan pepper, star anise, rice wine and salt into a pan. Cover and boil gently for 1 hour. Allow to cool, then remove the back and breast bones from the pigeons, keeping them as a piece. Heat 30ml (2 tablespoons) oil and stir-fry the red dates, pork, mushrooms and rice for 2 minutes. Add 275ml (½ pint, 1¼ cups) water, the soy sauce and salt and simmer for 15 minutes until almost dry. Fill the pigeons with this mixture and put them on a plate, breast-side down. Cover the plate with tinfoil and steam over a high heat for 1 hour. Arrange the pigeons breast-side up on a clean plate and serve.

Note: it is not necessary to bone these pigeons but they are harder to eat with the bones in.

94

Stuffed Roast Chicken

天厨鐵烤子母鷄

1.25kg (2½ lb) chicken
45ml (3 tablespoons) soy sauce
30ml (2 tablespoons) rice wine
10ml (2 teaspoons) Sichuan peppercorns
3 spring onions, finely chopped
4 slices ginger, finely chopped
4 dried mushrooms
50g (2 oz) bamboo shoots
60g (2½ oz) lean pork
60g (2½ oz) pickled cabbage
30ml (2 tablespoons) oil

Rub the chicken all over with 30ml (2 tablespoons) soy sauce, 15ml (1 tablespoon) rice wine, the Sichuan peppercorns, spring onions and ginger. Leave for 4 hours to marinate.

Soak the mushrooms in warm water for 30 minutes. Discard the stalks and finely slice the caps. Cut the bamboo shoots and the pork into fine shreds.

Heat the oil and stir-fry the bamboo shoots, mushrooms and pork. Add the pickled cabbage, 15ml (1 tablespoon) soy sauce and 15ml (1 tablespoon) rice wine and mix well. Stuff the chicken with this mixture and sew up the vent. Wrap it in tinfoil and roast in a moderate oven (180°C/350°F/Gas 4) for 2 hours. Unwrap and paint with the remaining marinade every 30 minutes during the cooking.

Steamed Chicken with Broccoli

碧綠上場鷄

1.25kg (2½ lb) chicken
3 spring onions, finely chopped
8 slices ginger, finely chopped
10ml (2 teaspoons) salt
10ml (2 teaspoons) ground Sichuan pepper
15ml (1 tablespoon) rice wine
2 petals star anise
250g (8 oz) broccoli
5ml (1 teaspoon) cornflour
sugar, salt and pepper

Rub the chicken all over with a mixture of spring onions, ginger, salt, ground Sichuan pepper and rice wine. Put the star anise inside the chicken. Leave for 2 hours. Trim and wash the broccoli. Tear into florets. Mix the cornflour into a paste with 15ml (1 tablespoon) water.

Steam the chicken on a deep plate for 1 hour over full heat. Then chop into pieces and arrange on a serving dish. Reserve the cooking liquor. Cook the broccoli in boiling water until cooked, then drain and arrange round the chicken. Boil the reserved chicken stock. Season to taste and thicken with the cornflour paste. Pour over the chicken and serve.

Drunken Chicken

500g (1 lb) chicken (half a chicken)
5ml (1 teaspoon) ground Sichuan pepper
15ml (1 tablespoon) salt
200ml (⅓ pint, 1 cup) rice wine
5ml (1 teaspoon) ginger juice
250g (8 oz) cauliflower
5ml (1 teaspoon) salt

Rub the chicken all over with the salt and ground Sichuan pepper. Leave for 12 hours to marinate. Wash and break the cauliflower into florets.

Steam the chicken for 45 minutes and leave to cool. Chop into bite-sized pieces and put in a bowl with the rice wine and ginger juice. Leave for 48 hours covered in the refrigerator. Then boil the cauliflower in salted water until it is just cooked. Drain and cool. Serve with the chicken arranged on a plate surrounded by the cauliflower.

97

Braised Chicken with Chestnuts

白果栗子鷄

15 dried chestnuts
500g (1 lb) chicken legs
4 spring onions
30ml (2 tablespoons) oil
3 slices ginger
5ml (1 teaspoon) salt
15ml (1 tablespoon) rice wine
15ml (1 tablespoon) soy sauce
15 canned gingko nuts

Soak the dried chestnuts overnight and then simmer in boiling water for 20 minutes. Chop the chicken legs into bite-sized pieces. Cut the spring onions into 1cm (½-inch) lengths.

Heat the oil in a pan and stir-fry the ginger and onions for 15 seconds. Add the chicken and salt and fry until it changes colour. Pour in the rice wine and soy sauce with 150ml (¼ pint, ⅔ cup) water. Mix well and add the chestnuts and gingko nuts. Simmer for 20 minutes, then adjust the seasoning to taste before serving.

Stir-fried Chicken with Red-in-snow

雪菜鷄丁

200g (7 oz) chicken breast
200g (7 oz) canned red-in-snow
1 spring onion
5ml (1 teaspoon) sugar
30ml (2 tablespoons) oil
10ml (2 teaspoons) soy sauce
50g (2 oz) frozen peas
10ml (2 teaspoons) rice wine
sugar to taste

Dice the chicken into 1cm (½-inch) cubes. Rinse the red-in-snow and chop finely. Chop the spring onion finely.

Fry the red-in-snow in a dry frying-pan with the sugar for 3 minutes. Then lift out. Clean the frying-pan and heat the oil. Stir-fry the onion, then the chicken. Add the soy sauce, then the peas and red-in-snow. Mix well and season to taste with rice wine and sugar before serving.
Note: this dish is good with fried rice. Stir-fry cooked rice in oil and add the chicken and red-in-snow.

Crispy Fried Chicken

江南脆皮鷄

500g (1 lb) poussin or small chicken
5ml (1 teaspoon) wuxiang
5ml (1 teaspoon) salt
5ml (1 teaspoon) ground Sichuan pepper
5ml (1 teaspoon) vinegar
5ml (1 teaspoon) clear honey
5ml (1 teaspoon) cornflour
oil for deep frying

Rub the chicken all over with a mixture of the salt, *wuxiang* and ground pepper. Leave in a cold place for 6 hours.

Paint the chicken with the prepared syrup and hang in a moving current of air for 3 hours to dry. Then put the chicken into hot oil, lower the heat and fry for 7 minutes. Lift out and drain. Re-heat the oil and return the chicken to the oil for another 2 minutes to make the skin crisp. Chop into pieces and serve hot with a peppersalt dip (see page 84).

Chicken Stewed with Mussels

蚬菜燉鶏

1.5kg (3 lb) boiling fowl
2 spring onions
2 slices ginger
60ml (4 tablespoons) rice wine
20 frozen mussels
500g (1 lb) Chinese cabbage
150g (5 oz) raw ham
5ml (1 teaspoon) salt
salt and pepper to taste

Put the spring onions and ginger inside the chicken with 30ml (2 tablespoons) rice wine. De-frost the mussels and marinate in 30ml (2 tablespoons) rice wine. Wash and cut the Chinese cabbage into 4cm (1½-inch) lengths.

Put the chicken into a pan with sufficient water to cover. Add 5ml (1 teaspoon) salt and bring to the boil. Skim the foam from the surface, reduce the heat and cover the pan. Simmer for 1½ hours. Then add the ham and Chinese cabbage and simmer for another hour. Add more water when necessary. Finally add the mussels and their marinade and simmer for 20 minutes. Adjust the seasoning and serve in an earthenware pot.

Stir-fried Chicken with Vegetables

辣子鶏丁

400g (14 oz) chicken without
    bones
30ml (2 tablespoons) rice wine
15ml (1 tablespoon) cornflour
5ml (1 teaspoon) salt
125g (4 oz) bamboo shoots
1 green pepper
2 chillis
2 spring onions
10ml (2 teaspoons) chilli-bean
    sauce
10ml (2 teaspoons) sugar
15ml (1 tablespoon) soy sauce
10ml (2 teaspoons) rice vinegar
5ml (1 teaspoon) sesame oil
oil for deep frying

Cut the chicken into 2cm (1-inch) cubes. Marinate with 15ml
(1 tablespoon) rice wine, 7.5ml (1½ teaspoons) cornflour
and 5ml (1 teaspoon) salt for 30 minutes. Cut the bamboo
shoots into small slices. De-seed and cut the pepper into
2cm (1-inch) slices and cut the spring onions into 4cm
(1½-inch) lengths. De-seed and slice the chillis.

    Heat the oil and deep-fry the chicken for 2 minutes. Lift
out and drain. Heat 30ml (2 tablespoons) oil in a pan and
stir-fry the onions and chillis. Add the bamboo and pepper
and continue to stir-fry for another minute. Add the chicken,
then the chilli-bean sauce, soy sauce, rice vinegar, sugar,
remaining rice wine and the cornflour mixed with 15ml (1
tablespoon) water. Stir well and serve sprinkled with sesame
oil.

Smoked Duck

樟茶鴨

2kg (4 lb) duck
30ml (2 tablespoons) ground
    Sichuan pepper
45ml (3 tablespoons) salt
125g (4 oz) rice
125g (4 oz) Indian tea
125g (4 oz) brown sugar
20 spring onions, cut into
    brushes
45ml (3 tablespoons) sweet
    bean sauce

Rub the duck all over with the pepper and salt. Hang up to
dry in an airy place for about 3 hours.

    Put the rice, tea and sugar in the bottom of a heavy *old*
pan, and stand a trivet over them. Put the duck on the trivet
and cover with a close-fitting lid. Stand over a moderate heat
for 15 minutes. Then turn the duck and leave closely
covered for another 10 minutes. Put the duck in a steamer
and steam for 1½ hours over a high heat. Chop into pieces
and serve with onion brushes and a dip of sweet bean sauce.

Stir-fried Chicken in Chilli-oil

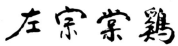

400g (14 oz) chicken
1 egg
15ml (1 tablespoon) soy sauce
10ml (2 teaspoons) rice wine
15ml (1 tablespoon) cornflour
5 chillis
5ml (1 teaspoon) crushed garlic
10ml (2 teaspoons) minced ginger
5ml (1 teaspoon) rice vinegar
5ml (1 teaspoon) sesame oil

Cut the chicken into bite-sized pieces and marinate with the egg, 10ml (2 teaspoons) soy sauce, the rice wine and cornflour. Cut each chilli into half. De-seed and cut each piece in two lengthwise.

Heat the oil and deep-fry the chicken for 5 minutes. Lift out and drain. Heat a pan with 60ml (4 tablespoons) oil and stir-fry the chillis. Then add the garlic and ginger, the remaining teaspoon of soy sauce and the vinegar. Mix in the chicken pieces and stir well to coat in the chilli oil. Serve sprinkled with sesame oil.

Roast Chicken

豆醬焗雞

1kg (2 lb) chicken
15ml (1 tablespoon) oil
30ml (2 tablespoons) hoisin sauce
15ml (1 tablespoon) sugar
15ml (1 tablespoon) soy sauce
15ml (1 tablespoon) rice wine
10ml (2 teaspoons) salt
3 spring onions
4 slices ginger
1 piece pork fat

Heat the oil in a pan and mix in the *hoisin* sauce, sugar, soy sauce, rice wine and salt. Allow to cool and then paint the chicken all over with this mixture.

Put the spring onions and ginger inside the chicken and leave to marinate for 6 hours.

Put the pork in the bottom of an ovenproof casserole, and put the chicken on top. Cover closely and roast for 1 hour at 190°C/375°F/Gas 5. Chop the chicken and arrange on a plate. Pour the cooking juices over it and serve.

107

Phoenix Claws Soup

筍菇
鳳爪湯

14 chickens' feet
8 dried mushrooms
3 squares beancurd
50g (2 oz) raw ham
2 spring onions
2 slices ginger
1 litre (1¾ pints, 1 quart) chicken stock
15ml (1 tablespoon) rice wine
salt to taste

Wash the chickens' feet well, then dip them separately in boiling water for 15 seconds. Peel off the scaly outside skin and remove the nails. Cut each foot in half crosswise. Soak the mushrooms in warm water for 30 minutes, then discard the hard stalk. Cut each square of beancurd in half.

Cut the ham into thin slices.

Put the chickens' feet with the onion, ginger, stock and rice wine into a pan. Bring to the boil, skim off any foam that rises then turn down the heat, cover the pan and simmer for 45 minutes. Add the mushrooms, ham and beancurd and simmer for a further 30 minutes. Adjust the seasoning and serve.

Double Chicken Threads

350g (12 oz) chicken breast
45ml (3 tablespoons) rice wine
5ml (1 teaspoon) salt
300ml (½ pint, 1 cup) chicken stock
2 dried mushrooms
2 spring onions
25ml (1½ tablespoons) cornflour
2 egg whites
30ml (2 tablespoons) frozen peas
oil for deep frying

Divide the chicken into two halves. Cut one half into thin shreds and marinate with 15ml (1 tablespoon) rice wine, 10ml (2 teaspoons) cornflour and the salt.

Cook the other chicken half in the stock with 15ml (1 tablespoon) rice wine for 20 minutes. Leave to cool, then reserve the stock and tear the chicken into shreds.

Soak the mushrooms in warm water for 30 minutes. Then discard the hard stalks and shred the caps.

Chop the spring onions finely.

Mix the remaining cornflour with 30ml (2 tablespoons) water.

Lightly beat the egg whites and mix them with the marinating uncooked chicken. Heat the oil to hot and deep-fry the chicken for 30 seconds. Lift out and drain. Heat a pan with 30ml (2 tablespoons) oil and stir-fry the onions and mushrooms. Add the reserved stock, 15ml (1 tablespoon) rice wine and the peas. Bring to the boil and mix in both halves of the chicken. Adjust the seasoning and thicken with the cornflour paste. Serve.

Spiced Chicken Wings

紅燒鷄翅

10 chicken wings
45ml (3 tablespoons) soy sauce
2ml (½ teaspoon) salt
30ml (2 tablespoons) rice wine
2 spring onions
3 slices ginger
15ml (1 tablespoon) sugar
pinch wuxiang
5ml (1 teaspoon) sesame oil
oil for deep frying

Marinate the chicken wings in 15ml (1 tablespoon) soy sauce, the salt and 15ml (1 tablespoon) rice wine for an hour.

Heat the oil and deep-fry the chicken wings for 4 minutes. Drain well. Then put them in a pan with the onions, ginger, remaining soy sauce and rice wine, sugar and *wuxiang*. Cover with water and bring to the boil. Turn down the heat and simmer for 40 minutes, by which time the chicken should be very tender and the liquid almost gone. During the cooking turn the chicken in the sauce. Serve sprinkled with sesame oil.

Curried Chicken

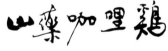

750g (1½ lb) chicken, with
    bones
150g (5 oz) onion
250g (8 oz) yam, or sweet
    potato
2 slices ginger
15ml (1 tablespoon) curry
    powder
15ml (1 tablespoon) soy sauce
5ml (1 teaspoon) salt
5ml (1 teaspoon) sugar
60ml (4 tablespoons) oil

Chop the chicken into 5cm (2-inch) pieces. Chop the onion finely. Peel the yam and cut into bite-sized pieces. Rub with a little salt, then boil in water for 5 minutes. Discard the water and put into fresh water to boil for a further 10 minutes. Lift out and drain.

Heat 30ml (2 tablespoons) oil in a pan and fry the ginger and chicken for 4 minutes. Then lift out. Clean the pan and re-heat with 30ml (2 tablespoons) oil. Stir-fry the onion and curry powder and then return the chicken. Add the soy sauce, salt and sugar and 500ml (1 pint) water. Simmer for 30 minutes then add the yams. Continue simmering for another 10 minutes and serve.

Clay-baked Chicken

富貴雞

1.75kg (3½ lb) chicken
4 spring onions
5 slices ginger
15ml (1 tablespoon) rice wine
15ml (1 tablespoon) soy sauce
15ml (1 tablespoon) oyster sauce
125g (4 oz) belly of pork
75g (3 oz) bamboo shoots
4 chillis
15ml (1 tablespoon) oil
15ml (1 tablespoon) Tianjin pickled cabbage
lard

2kg (4 lb) clay*
4 sheets greaseproof paper
4 lotus leaves

Rub the chicken all over with a mixture of 2 spring onions (finely chopped), chopped ginger, rice wine, soy sauce and oyster sauce. Mince the pork, bamboo shoots, chillis and 2 spring onions and mix together.

Stir-fry this mixture in the oil with the Tianjin pickled vegetable, then use to stuff the chicken. Sew up the vent securely. Grease the paper with the lard and wrap up the chicken. Then wrap the paper parcel in lotus leaves softened in boiling water and tie firmly so that no juice can escape during cooking.

Soften the clay with water and press it out flat on a wet cloth. Lay the wrapped chicken in the centre and mould the clay firmly round the chicken. Remove the wet cloth and bake the chicken at 70°C/150°F/Gas ¼ for 4½ hours. Break open the clay, untie the parcel, cut the stitches from the vent, and serve.

*Note: alternatively, wrap the chicken in aluminium foil, and replace the clay with 2.5kg (5 lb) flour. Mix flour in water to make dough; wrap around foil. Bake at 190°C/375°F/Gas 5 for 2 hours. Serve.

Pigeons in Ramekins

竹節鴿盅

5 pigeons
250g (8 oz) fat pork
75g (3 oz) frozen scallops
45ml (3 tablespoons) rice wine
8 water chestnuts
5ml (1 teaspoon) salt
30ml (2 tablespoons) soy sauce

Skin and remove the breasts from the pigeons. Mince them with the pork. De-frost and marinate the scallops in 30ml (2 tablespoons) rice wine for 20 minutes. Reserve the marinade and shred the scallops. Mince the water chestnuts. Mix all the ingredients together and blend well. Fill 12 small ramekins with the mixture.

Steam the ramekins over a high heat for 40 minutes. Turn out into soup bowls and serve hot.

Note: if you do not have ramekins use tea-cups.

113

Peking Duck

北平烤鸭

2kg (4 lb) duckling
5ml (1 teaspoon) maltose
25ml (5 teaspoons) boiling water
125g (4 oz) sweet bean sauce
40g (1 ½ oz) crystal sugar
spring onions, cut into brushes

Remove the oil sac from behind the duck's tail and pour boiling water all over its exterior. Dry carefully. Mix a syrup of maltose and boiling water and paint this over the duck. Hang the duck up to dry in a draughty place, or hang in front of a cold fan, for 4 hours.

Mix the sweet bean sauce with the sugar and 175ml (⅓ pint, ¾ cup) water and simmer until the sugar has dissolved. Allow to cool.

Hang the duck from the top of a pre-heated oven, 220°C/425°F/Gas 7, and put a drip tray underneath. Cook for 20 minutes, then reduce the temperature to 190°C/375°F/Gas 6 and roast for a further 40 minutes. Serve sliced very thinly with sweet bean sauce and lotus pancakes.

Lotus Pancakes

Mix 250g (8 oz) plain flour with 150ml (¼ pint, ½ cup) boiling water into a dough. Knead well. Divide into 14 portions and roll out into 10cm (4-inch) circles. Paint with sesame oil and sandwich two circles together before rolling both out into 15cm (6-inch) circles. Heat a dry frying-pan over a low heat and cook the double pancakes, turning once. Separate and serve.

114

Steamed Pigeons

杞子
燉鴿

12 pigeons
5ml (1 teaspoon) kouchi
5ml (1 teaspoon) salt
2 slices ginger

Scald the pigeons in boiling water for 2 minutes, then rinse well. Put the pigeons with the *kouchi*, salt, ginger and 400ml (14 fl oz, 1¾ cups) water into a bowl. Cover the bowl with tinfoil. Steam the pigeons for 3 hours, or until tender. Serve in the bowl in which they were cooked.
Note: *kouchi* are sometimes called Chinese medlars. Sold mainly for medicinal purposes, they are very expensive.

Salted Chicken with Black Beans

豉油鹹鷄

750g (1½ lb) chicken (half a
   chicken)
25ml (1½ tablespoons) salt
5ml (1 teaspoon) ground
   Sichuan pepper
3 spring onions
2 slices ginger
15ml (1 tablespoon) fermented
   black beans
45ml (3 tablespoons) rice wine
45ml (3 tablespoons) oil

Rub the chicken all over with a mixture of the pepper and
salt. Leave the chicken for 2 days in the refrigerator to
marinate. Finely chop the spring onions with the fermented
black beans and ginger.
   After 2 days rinse the chicken. Pat dry and put on a plate
with the rice wine. Steam for 15 minutes. Meanwhile heat
the oil and stir-fry the onions, black beans and ginger. Spoon
over the chicken and steam for a further 30 minutes. Chop
into bite-sized pieces and serve.

Chicken and Beancurd Salad

鷄絲拌粉皮

200g (7 oz) chicken breast
15ml (1 tablespoon) rice wine
1 spring onion
2 slices ginger
1 iceberg lettuce
150g (5 oz) carrot
4 squares beancurd
30ml (2 tablespoons) soy sauce
15ml (1 tablespoon) sesame oil
5ml (1 teaspoon) sugar
salt

Marinate the chicken in the rice wine and a pinch of salt. Cut
the spring onions into 2cm (1-inch) lengths and put them
with the ginger on the chicken. Steam the chicken for 25
minutes, then tear in shreds. Wash the lettuce and shred
finely, mix with a pinch of salt. Peel the carrot, shred and mix
with a little salt. Press the beancurd shreds and then cut into
matchstick shreds.
   Lay the beancurd shreds on a plate, cover with the lettuce
and chicken shreds and put the carrot on top. Sprinkle with a
dressing made from soy sauce, sesame oil and sugar and
serve.

116

Chicken and Ham Pot

鶏火
冬瓜湯

750g (1½ lb) chicken (half a chicken)
300g (10 oz) lean raw ham
3 dried mushrooms
1 spring onion
2 slices ginger
45ml (3 tablespoons) rice wine
5ml (1 teaspoon) salt
1 can winter melon

Scald chicken in boiling water for 2 minutes, then rinse. Rinse ham in hot water. Soak dried mushrooms in hot water for 30 minutes then discard hard stalks. Cut the spring onions into 1cm (½-inch) lengths.

Put the chicken, ham, onion, ginger and rice wine into a pan with just enough boiling water to cover. Skim if necessary, cover with a lid and simmer for an hour. Then add the mushrooms and drained winter melon. Season with salt to taste and simmer for 10 more minutes. If you want more soup add another 200ml (⅓ pint, 1 cup) water to the pan with the mushrooms.

118

Steamed Chicken with Green Onions

葱油淋鷄

1.25kg (2½ lb) roasting chicken
10ml (2 teaspoons) salt
1 piece ginger
15ml (1 tablespoon) rice wine
1 spring onion
30ml (2 tablespoons) shredded spring onions
30ml (2 tablespoons) shredded ginger
40ml (2½ tablespoons) oil
5ml (1 teaspoon) cornflour (optional)

Rub the chicken all over with the ginger dipped in the salt and rice wine. Place the remaining rice wine, salt and ginger with 1 spring onion inside the chicken. Leave to marinate for 30 minutes. Mix the cornflour into a paste with 10ml (2 teaspoons) water.

Steam the chicken for 1 hour, then chop into small pieces; reserve the cooking juices. Arrange the chicken on a plate and pour over the reserved juices. Sprinkle the shredded onions and ginger over the chicken. Heat the oil to very hot and pour on top of the onion and ginger shreds. Serve at once.

Note: an alternative method of serving is to heat the reserved cooking juices, onion and ginger shreds in a pan with the oil. Thicken with the cornflour paste and pour over the chicken.

Five-colour shreds

五世其昌

7 large dried mushrooms
300g (10 oz) chicken breast
35ml (2½ tablespoons) rice wine
1 spring onion
1 slice ginger
200g (7 oz) cucumber
10ml (2 teaspoons) salt
1 carrot
250g (8 oz) bamboo shoots
10ml (2 teaspoons) soy sauce
pinch of sugar

Soak the mushrooms in 250ml (½ pint) warm water for 30 minutes. Then discard the hard stalks. Reserve the soaking water. Marinate the chicken in 30ml (2 tablespoons) rice wine, the spring onion cut into 1cm (½-inch) lengths and the ginger shredded. Rub the cucumber in the salt and leave for 30 minutes. Rinse and shred. Peel and shred the carrot. Boil the bamboo shoots in water for 20 minutes, then shred.

Steam the mushrooms in the soaking water with 5ml (1 teaspoon) rice wine, the soy sauce and sugar for 30 minutes. Steam the chicken in its marinade for 30 minutes, then allow to cool. Cut the mushrooms and chicken into shreds. Arrange the different-coloured shreds around a plate and serve with dishes of soy sauce and sesame oil as a dip.

Note: substitute beansprouts for the bamboo shoots if you prefer. This dish represents 'good luck' and is served at wedding banquets.

Steamed Chicken with Ham

金華玉樹鷄

1.25kg (2½ lb) chicken
3 spring onions
3 slices ginger
5ml (1 teaspoon) salt
45ml (3 tablespoons) rice wine
200g (7 oz) raw ham
25ml (1½ tablespoons) sugar
5ml (1 teaspoon) soy sauce
5ml (1 teaspoon) cornflour
a few choisam leaves (optional)

Rub the chicken inside and out with a mixture of 2 finely chopped spring onions, 2 slices of ginger (chopped), the salt and 20ml (1½ tablespoons) rice wine. Cut the ham into slices 1cm (½-inch) wide and 5cm (2 inches) long and marinate with 20ml (1½ tablespoons) rice wine, 1 finely chopped spring onion, 1 slice ginger and the sugar. Mix the cornflour into a paste with 10ml (2 teaspoons) water.

Steam the chicken in its marinade for 1 hour and the ham in a separate bowl for 30 minutes. Bone the chicken, retaining the skin and cut the meat into 5cm (2-inch)-long slices. Arrange on a plate with the slices of ham between the chicken slices. Put the cooking juices from the ham and chicken into a pan and bring to the boil. Season with soy sauce and thicken with the cornflour paste. Pour over the chicken and serve garnished with a few pieces of braised choisam.

Steamed Sea Bream with Clams

清蒸魚鮮

750g (1½ lb) sea bream (or
   pomfret)
10ml (2 teaspoons) salt
30ml (2 tablespoons) rice wine
16 live clams
6 spring onions
15ml (1 tablespoon) grated
   ginger
45ml (3 tablespoons) oil

Wash the fish clean and score both sides with 3-4 cuts.
Sprinkle with salt, inside and out, then with rice wine. Leave
to marinate. Soak the clams in lightly salted water for 2
hours, stirring from time to time. Rinse well and arrange
round the fish. Cut the spring onions into 7cm (3-inch)
lengths. Put them on top of the fish with the ginger.
   Steam the fish and clams over a moderate heat for 20
minutes. Then lift off the clams and discard any which are
closed. Heat the oil in a pan and pour over the fish. Continue
to steam for another 5 minutes, or until the fish's eye is
puffed up. Serve surrounded by the clams and garnished
with mushroom, carrot dice and lightly boiled green peas.

Fried Prawn Balls with Wood Ears
and Spring Onions

3 pieces wood ears
6 spring onions
15ml (1 tablespoon) soy sauce
12 fried prawn balls (see page
   125)
30ml (2 tablespoons) oil

Soak the wood ears in warm water for 20 minutes. Then
rinse and cut into bite-sized pieces. Cut the spring onions
into 4cm (1½-inch) lengths. Prepare and fry the prawn balls.
   Heat the oil in a pan and stir-fry the wood ears for 30
seconds. Add the spring onions and continue stir-frying for
another minute. Season with soy sauce and turn out on to a
serving plate. Arrange the prawn balls on top and serve at
once.

Steamed Eggs with Clams

蛤蜊燉蛋

12 live clams
2 spring onions
2 slices ginger
30ml (2 tablespoons) rice wine
10ml (2 teapoons) salt
3 large eggs
10ml (2 teaspoons) soy sauce
10ml (2 teaspoons) grated ginger

Wash the clams thoroughly and soak them in lightly salted water for 3 hours. Rinse and drain. Dice the white parts of the spring onions; reserve the green leaves.

Boil 250ml (½ pint, 1¼ cups) water and add the spring onion leaves, slices of ginger, rice wine and salt. Put in the clams, cover the pan and return to the boil. Then lift out the clams, discard those that are closed and put the open clams in a bowl. When they are cold, beat the eggs and pour them over the clams. Add the soy sauce and 425ml (¾ pint, 1¾ cups) cold water. Steam over a low heat until the egg is set (about 30 minutes). Sprinkle the diced spring onion and grated ginger over the bowl before serving.

Fried Prawn Balls

炸蝦球

400g (14 oz) raw prawns
50g (2 oz) pork bacon fat
1 small egg white
15ml (1 tablespoon) rice wine
5ml (1 teaspoon) ginger juice
5ml (1 teaspoon) finely chopped spring onion
15ml (1 tablespoon) cornflour
oil for deep frying

Shell the prawns and remove the dark digestive cords running through their bodies. Mince the pork fat. Put the prawns and pork fat into a food processor and blend to a smooth paste. Add the egg white, rice wine, ginger juice, chopped spring onions and cornflour and blend well.

Heat the oil to very hot, then lower the heat. Shape the prawn balls by squeezing the mixture in your left hand up between the index finger and thumb. Lift the balls off with a spoon and drop into the hot oil. Fry until golden brown over a moderate heat. Lift out and drain. Serve with a peppersalt dip, see page 84.

River Fish Soup

乾尾川瑒

1 small wrasse or carp
350g (12 oz) white radish
3 spring onions
75g (5 tablespoons) cornflour
4 slices ginger
600ml (1 pint, 3 cups) well-
    seasoned stock
15ml (1 tablespoon) rice wine
150ml (¼ pint, ¾ cup) milk
salt and pepper
15ml (1 tablespoon) chopped
    coriander
oil for deep frying

Clean, scale and wash the fish; cut into 8cm (3-inch) slices. Peel and shred the white radish. Cut the spring onions into 2cm (1-inch) lengths. Mix 10ml (2 teaspoons) cornflour with 15ml (1 tablespoon) water.

Roll the fish in the dry cornflour and deep-fry for 7 minutes. Drain well. Boil the stock and put in the spring onions, ginger and rice wine. Add the fish, then the white radish shreds. Pour in the milk. Adjust the seasoning and thicken with cornflour. Serve with the chopped coriander.

Fried Carp

乾燒鯉魚

1 small wrasse or carp
30ml (2 tablespoons) soy sauce
30ml (2 tablespoons) cornflour
25g (1 oz) pork
5 slices ginger
3 spring onions
2 chillis
2 cloves garlic
15ml (1 tablespoon) rice wine
5ml (1 teaspoon) vinegar
450ml (¾ pint, 2½ cups) stock
5ml (1 teaspoon) sugar
5ml (1 teaspoon) sesame oil
oil for deep frying

Clean, scale and wash the fish. Remove head and tail and score the body in a diamond pattern. Marinate with 15ml (1 tablespoon) soy sauce. Cut the pork into matchstick shreds. Chop the spring onions, ginger, chillis and garlic. Mix 10ml (2 teaspoons) cornflour with 15ml (1 tablespoon) water.

Heat the oil to very hot. Dust the fish with the remaining cornflour and deep-fry for 2 minutes. Heat 30ml (2 tablespoons) oil in a big pan and stir-fry the onions, ginger, garlic and chillis. Add the rice wine, vinegar, stock and sugar, then put in the fish and pork. Simmer until the fish is cooked. Lift out the fish and thicken the gravy with the cornflour paste. Pour over the fish and serve sprinkled with sesame oil.

127

Sichuan Fish Soup

川揚青魚

600g (1 ¼ lb) bass (middle section)
300g (10 oz) Chinese cabbage
15ml (1 tablespoon) salt
45ml (3 tablespoons) vodka
2 spring onions
2 slices ginger
15ml (1 tablespoon) melted lard
coriander
salt and pepper

Scale, wash and cut the fish into 4cm (1½-inch) pieces. Marinate with the salt and vodka in a covered dish in the refrigerator for 12 hours, turning from time to time. Rinse the fish before cooking. Wash the Chinese cabbage and cut into bite-sized pieces. Cut the spring onions into 2cm (1-inch) lengths.

Boil the cabbage, fish, onions and ginger in 570ml (1 pint, 3 cups) water for 10 minutes. Check the seasoning, pour over the melted lard and serve garnished with sprigs of coriander.

Fish Pot

砂鍋
頭尾

750g (1½ lb) baby haddock
5ml (1 teaspoon) salt
15ml (1 tablespoon) soy sauce
30ml (2 tablespoons) rice wine
3 squares beancurd
150g (5 oz) fresh button mushrooms
3 wood ears
2 chillis
4 spring onions
2 slices ginger
3 garlic shoots
10ml (2 teaspoons) cornflour
60ml (4 tablespoons) oil

Clean, scale and wash the fish. Cut into 5cm (2-inch) pieces. Cut the head in half lengthwise. Marinate with salt, soy sauce and rice wine. Cut the beancurd into 2cm (1-inch) cubes. Wipe the mushrooms. Soak the wood ears in warm water for 20 minutes. Then rinse and cut into pieces. Slice the chillis. Cut the spring onions into 2cm (1-inch) lengths. Slice the garlic slantwise. Mix the cornflour with 15ml (1 tablespoon) water.

Heat the oil and stir-fry the chillis for 15 seconds. Lift out. Stir-fry the onion and ginger in the same oil. Add the fish and stir-fry for 2 minutes. Put the fish, onions, ginger and remaining marinade with the mushrooms and wood ears into a casserole. Add 570ml (1 pint, 3 cups) water and bring to the boil. Add the chillis and beancurd and simmer for 10 minutes. Check the seasoning, thicken with the cornflour paste and scatter the garlic over the top. Serve.

129

Steamed Eels with Chinese Medlars

杞子蒸河鰻

1kg (2 lb) freshwater eel
10ml (2 teaspoons) salt
150ml (¼ pint) vodka
10ml (2 teaspoons) kouchi
    (optional)
15g (½ oz) ginger
3 spring onions

Cut off the eel's head and score the body deeply every 4cm (1½ inches). Do not cut right through. Marinate with the salt, vodka and *kouchi*. Shred the ginger and spring onions finely and put over the eel.

Steam the eel in the marinade until cooked (about 15 minutes). Serve hot.

Note: *kouchi*, sometimes called Chinese medlars, are sold mainly for medicinal purposes and are expensive.

Stir-fried Squid

韮苗墨魚

600g (1¼ lb) squid
300g (10 oz) leeks (inside
    leaves)
2 wood ears
2 spring onions
2 chillis
2 slices ginger
1 clove garlic, crushed
5ml (1 teaspoon) salt
10ml (2 teaspoons) soy sauce
60ml (4 tablespoons) oil

Clean and score the squid (see page 23). Cut into 2cm (1-inch) strips. Blanch in boiling water for 1 minute, then lift out and drain. Wash and cut the inside leek leaves into 7cm (3-inch) lengths. Soak the wood ears until soft, then shred. Cut the spring onions into 1cm (½-inch) lengths and slice the chillis.

Heat 30ml (2 tablespoons) oil in a pan and stir-fry the leeks with a little salt until soft. Lift out and clean the pan. Heat 30ml (2 tablespoons) more oil and stir-fry the spring onions and ginger. Add the chillis, garlic and wood ears. Bring to the boil with 150ml (¼ pint, ¾ cup) water and season with salt and soy sauce. Add the squid. Arrange the leeks on a plate and pour the squid and its sauce over them.

Stir-fried Squid with Bean Sprouts

銀芽
炒鮮魷

300g (10 oz) fresh squid
400g (15 oz) bean sprouts
1 chilli
1 spring onion
15ml (1 tablespoon) skinned broad beans
15ml (1 tablespoon) soy sauce
15ml (1 tablespoon) rice wine
5ml (1 teaspoon) salt
2ml (½ teaspoon) sesame oil
oil for deep frying

Pick over and rinse the bean sprouts. Prepare the squid according to the instructions on page 23. De-seed and shred the chilli. Cut the spring onion into 1cm (½-inch) lengths.

Heat the oil and stir-fry the squid rings for 10 seconds. Lift out and drain. Blanch the bean sprouts in boiling water for 30 seconds, then refresh in cold water and drain. Heat 30ml (2 tablespoons) oil in a pan and stir-fry the chilli shreds for 30 seconds. Lift out. Then stir-fry the spring onion and broad beans. Add the bean sprouts and stir-fry for a moment before adding the squid. Season with soy sauce, rice wine and salt and serve garnished with the chilli shreds and sprinkled with sesame oil.

134

Prawn and Pork Broth

蝦仁肉絲羹

250g (8 oz) cooked shelled prawns
1 egg white
5ml (1 teaspoons) rice wine
30ml (2 tablespoons) cornflour
200g (7 oz) lean pork
150g (5 oz) cabbage heart
2 spring onions
25g (1 oz) carrot
45ml (3 tablespoons) oil
2 slices ginger
15ml (1 tablespoon) soy sauce
750ml (1¼ pints, 3 cups) stock

Marinate the prawns in egg white, 2ml (½ teaspoon) salt, 15ml (1 tablespoon) rice wine and 7.5ml (1½ teaspoons) cornflour. Cut the pork into thin slices and marinate with 3ml (½ teaspoon) salt, 15ml (1 tablespoon) rice wine, and 7.5ml (1½ teaspoons) cornflour. Wash and shred the cabbage. Cut the spring onions into ½cm (¼-inch) lengths and dice the carrot. Mix 15ml (1 tablespoon) cornflour with 30ml (2 tablespoons) water.

Heat the oil in a pan and stir-fry the onion, ginger and carrot. Add the cabbage shreds, stir-fry for 1 minute, then lift out. Put in the prawns and stir-fry for 30 seconds, then add the pork. Stir-fry before adding the soy sauce and then the stock. Mix well, add the cabbage and bring to the boil. Thicken with cornflour paste and serve.

Sweet and Sour Crispy Fish

糖醋脆黄鱼

600g (1¼ lb) baby haddock or yellow croaker	12 raw prawns
40ml (2½ tablespoons) soy sauce	75ml (5 tablespoons) cornflour
	2 spring onions, chopped
45ml (3 tablespoons) rice wine	3 slices ginger
2 dried mushrooms	1 clove garlic, crushed
15ml (1 tablespoon) skinned broad beans	30ml (2 tablespoons) vinegar
	30ml (2 tablespoons) sugar
15ml (1 tablespoon) diced carrot	salt
	oil for deep frying

Scale, wash and score the fish on both sides. Rub with a little salt and marinate in 20ml (1½ tablespoons) soy sauce and 20ml (1½ tablespoons) rice wine. Soak the mushrooms until soft. Discard the stalks and dice the caps. Par-boil the carrots and beans. Shell the prawns and de-vein but leave on their tails. Marinate in 25ml (1½ teaspoons) rice wine, 5ml (1 teaspoon) cornflour and a pinch of salt. Mix 10ml (2 teaspoons) cornflour with 15ml (1 tablespoon) water.

Heat the oil. Roll the fish in dry cornflour and deep-fry until cooked (about 7 minutes). Drain and keep warm. Heat 30ml (2 tablespoons) oil and stir-fry the ginger, onion and garlic. Add the mushrooms, then the prawns. Pour 150ml (¼ pint, ⅔ cup) water, the remaining soy sauce and rice wine, the sugar and vinegar. Mix well and bring to the boil. Add the carrots and beans and adjust the seasoning. Thicken with cornflour and pour over the fish. Serve.

Prawns and Broccoli

翡翠明蝦

14 cooked large prawns in their shells	30ml (2 tablespoons) vinegar
	15ml (1 tablespoon) sugar
250g (8 oz) broccoli	10ml (2 teaspoons) soy sauce
2 spring onions	salt
4 slices ginger	75ml (5 tablespoons, ¼ cup) oil
30ml (2 tablespoons) tomato purée	

Rinse the prawns and drain well. Wash and tear the broccoli into florets. Cut the spring onions into 1cm (½-inch) lengths.

Heat 45ml (3 tablespoons) oil in a pan and stir-fry the onion and ginger. Add the prawns and stir-fry for 1 minute before mixing in the tomato purée, vinegar, sugar and 75ml (5 tablespoons, ¼ cup) water. Keep warm. Heat 30ml (2 tablespoons) oil and stir-fry the broccoli with a pinch of salt. Add the soy sauce and serve with the prawns.

Steamed Fish with Mushrooms

清蒸鲳目鱼

2 fresh trout
30ml (2 tablespoons) rice wine
4 dried mushrooms
2 chillis
2 spring onions
2 slices ginger
2 button mushrooms
30ml (2 tablespoons) oil
salt

Clean and wash the trout. Rub inside and out with a little salt and marinate in the rice wine. Soak the dried mushrooms in warm water for 30 minutes, then discard the hard stalks and slice the caps finely. De-seed the chillis and cut them with the spring onions and ginger into fine shreds. Lay the shreds over the fish. Wipe and cut the fresh mushrooms into slices and put them on the fish.

Heat the oil and stir-fry the dried mushroom slices with a pinch of salt for 1 minute before tipping them with the oil over the fish. Steam the fish for 10 minutes. Serve.

138

Prawns with Meat Dumplings

鳳尾燕圓

200g (7 oz) cooked prawns with shells
6 water chestnuts
200g (7 oz) minced pork
3ml (½ teaspoon) salt
25ml (1½ tablespoons) rice wine
15ml (1 tablespoon) soy sauce
15ml (1 tablespoon) cornflour
16 wuntun skins
250g (8 oz) broccoli
1 spring onion
4 slices ginger
45ml (3 tablespoons) oil

Remove the prawn shells but leave on the tails. Mince the water chestnuts and mix them with the pork. Blend in the salt, 10ml (2 teaspoons) rice wine, 7.5ml (1½ teaspoons) soy sauce and 7.5ml (1½ teaspoons) cornflour. Beat well and divide into 16 portions. Wrap each portion in a *wuntun* skin. Wash and break the broccoli into florets. Cut the spring onion into 1cm (½-inch) lengths. Mix 7.5ml (1½ teaspoons) cornflour with 15ml (1 tablespoon) water.

Steam the wrapped meatballs for 20 minutes. Heat the oil in a pan and stir-fry the onion and ginger. Add the broccoli and stir-fry with a pinch of salt. Tip in 15ml (1 tablespoon) rice wine, 7.5ml (1½ teaspoons) soy sauce and 200ml (⅓ pint, 1 cup) water. Bring to the boil, add the prawns and meat dumplings and thicken with the cornflour paste. Serve.

Chilli-hot Fish

豆瓣
鯉魚

2 trout
cornflour
4 spring onions
5 slices ginger
4 cloves garlic
10ml (2 teaspoons) cornflour
15ml (1 tablespoon) chilli-bean sauce
15ml (1 tablespoon) soy sauce
2ml (½ teaspoon) salt
5ml (1 teaspoon) sugar
5ml (1 teaspoon) sesame oil
oil for deep frying

Clean and wash the trout and score on both sides. Finely chop the spring onions, ginger and garlic. Mix the cornflour with 15ml (1 tablespoon) water.

Heat the oil to hot and roll the fish in dry cornflour before deep-frying for 1 minute. Drain well. Heat 15ml (1 tablespoon) oil in a pan and stir-fry the onion (reserving a little of the chopped onion for garnish), ginger and garlic. Lower the heat and stir-fry the chilli-bean sauce before adding the soy, sugar, salt and 425ml (¾ pint, 2 cups) water. Bring to the boil and put in the fish. Simmer until cooked (about 3 minutes). Lift out the fish and place on a serving dish. Thicken the sauce with the cornflour paste and pour over the fish. Scatter over the reserved chopped onion and sesame oil before serving.

'Raw Fish' Soup

上湯泡魚生

450g (1 lb) halibut
4 lettuce leaves
8 sprigs coriander
1 fried batter stick (optional)
5ml (1 teaspoon) sesame seeds
5ml (1 teaspoon) finely chopped onion
450ml (¾ pint, 2 cups) good stock
15ml (1 tablespoon) rice wine
oil for deep frying

Skin and bone the fish and slice into paper-thin slices. Wash the lettuce and coriander. Tear the lettuce into shreds and remove the coriander stalks. Fry the batter stick until crisp, then drain and slice.

Arrange the lettuce in a bowl with the coriander. Put in the batter stick slices, then the fish slices. Sprinkle over the sesame seeds and chopped onion. Bring the stock to the boil, add the rice wine and quickly pour over the fish. Serve at once.

Spiced Fish

甘料薰鱼

450g (1 lb) haddock fillets
45ml (3 tablespoons) soy sauce
30ml (2 tablespoons) rice wine
15ml (1 tablespoon) grated
    ginger
3 spring onions
30ml (2 tablespoons) honey
pinch wuxiang
oil for deep frying

Cut the fillets lengthwise into strips about 4cm (1½ inches) wide and 13cm (5 inches) long. Marinate overnight in the soy sauce, rice wine, grated ginger and spring onions (finely chopped). Make a syrup of the honey, *wuxiang* and 150ml (¼ pint, ½ cup) boiling water.

Heat the oil to hot and carefully deep-fry the strips of fish for about 4 minutes; then immediately dip them in the spiced syrup. Serve at once, or serve cold.

Stuffed Fish

双鲜釀鲤鱼

750g (1½ lb) wrasse or small
    carp
15g (½ oz) dried shrimps
40g (2½ tablespoons) rice wine
125g (4 oz) minced pork
25ml (1½ tablespoons) soy
    sauce
5ml (1 teaspoon) salt
6 dried mushrooms
50g (2 oz) bamboo shoots
2 spring onions
2 slices ginger
15ml (1 tablespoon) cornflour
30ml (2 tablespoons) oil
300ml (½ pint, 1¼ cups) pork
    stock

Wash the fish. Soak the dried shrimps in 15ml (1 tablespoon) rice wine for 30 minutes. Then chop and mix with the minced pork, 7.5ml (½ tablespoon) soy sauce and the salt. Stuff into the fish. Soak the mushrooms for 30 minutes, then discard the hard stalks. Slice the bamboo shoots and cut the spring onion into 1cm (½-inch) lengths. Mix the cornflour with 30ml (2 tablespoons) water.

Steam the fish on a plate with the onions, ginger and 15ml (1 tablespoon) rice wine until cooked (about 40 minutes). Make a sauce by stir-frying the mushrooms in the oil, then add the bamboo shoots. Pour in the stock and bring to the boil. Thicken with the cornflour paste and pour over the fish before serving.

Stir-fried Oysters with Eggs

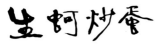

150g (5 oz) fresh shelled oysters
20ml (4 teaspoons) rice wine
15ml (1 tablespoon) cornflour
5ml (1 teaspoon) salt
3 spring onions
15ml (1 tablespoon) grated ginger
5 eggs
45ml (3 tablespoons) oil

Rinse the oysters to remove any pieces of shell and drain well. Marinate with 15ml (1 tablespoon) rice wine, the cornflour and 2ml (½ teaspoon) salt. Chop the white parts of the spring onions finely and mix into the oysters with the grated ginger. Beat the eggs well with 5ml (1 teaspoon) rice wine and a pinch of salt.

Heat the oil in a pan and quickly stir-fry the oysters. Then lift out and drain. Mix into the beaten egg and tip the mixture into the pan. Add more oil if necessary and stir-fry until the egg is just set. Serve.

Stir-fried Prawns with Pine Nuts

松子蝦仁

350g (12 oz) shelled prawns
½ egg white
2ml (½ teaspoon) salt
15ml (1 tablespoon) cornflour
15ml (1 tablespoon) rice wine
50g (2 oz) carrot
3 spring onions
25g (1 oz) pine nuts
3 slices ginger
50g (2 oz) frozen or canned sweetcorn
oil for deep frying

Marinate the prawns in the egg white, salt, cornflour and rice wine for 20 minutes. Peel and dice the carrot. Cut the spring onions into 1cm (½-inch) lengths. Heat 60ml (4 tablespoons) of oil and gently stir-fry the pine nuts for about 3 minutes. Lift out and drain. Deep-fry the prawns for 20 seconds in very hot oil, then drain.

   Heat 30ml (2 tablespoons) oil in a pan and stir-fry the onions and ginger. Then add the carrot and corn and stir-fry for another 3 minutes. Add the prawns and pine nuts and mix well. Serve.

Steamed Grouper

麒麟石斑魚

1 small grouper (or baby
    haddock)
15ml (1 tablespoon) rice wine
5ml (1 teaspoon) ground
    Sichuan pepper
10ml (2 teaspoons) grated
    ginger
10ml (2 teaspoons) finely
    chopped spring onion
pinch of wuxiang
5ml (1 teaspoon) sugar
15ml (1 tablespoon) cornflour
7 dried mushrooms
125g (4 oz) choisam
9 spring onions
10 slices ginger
150g (¼ pint, ½ cup) stock

Clean and wash the fish. Cut off its head, then fillet the body.
Cut the fillets into 5cm (2-inch) slices and marinate with the
rice wine, salt, Sichuan pepper, grated ginger, onions,
wuxiang, sugar and 7.5ml (½ tablespoon) cornflour.
Reserve the head and backbone. Soak the mushrooms in
warm water for 30 minutes, then discard the hard stalks and
cut the caps in halves. Wash and cook the *choisam* in boiling
water; drain well. Mix 20ml (1½ tablespoons) cornflour with
15ml (1 tablespoon) water.
    Put the onions and ginger on to a plate and on them
arrange the slices of fish with a piece of mushroom between
each slice. Put the fish head at one end and the backbone
over the fish slices. Steam until cooked (about 20 minutes).
Boil the stock, thicken with the cornflour paste and pour
over the fish. Garnish with *choisam* before serving.

West Lake Fish

清蒸鯧魚

1 small bream or pomfret
5ml (1 teaspoon) salt
8 spring onions
8 slices ginger
30ml (2 tablespoons) oil
30ml (2 tablespoons) soy sauce
15ml (1 tablespoon) rice wine

Wash and score the slices of the fish. Rub inside and out with
the salt. Finely shred the onions and ginger.
    Steam the fish over a high heat until cooked. Heat the oil
and stir-fry the ginger and onions. Add the soy sauce, rice
wine and the juices from cooking the fish. Pour over the fish
and serve.

Smoked Fish

烟燻
黄鱼

1 small sea bass
5ml (1 teaspoon) salt
15ml (1 tablespoon) rice wine
15ml (1 tablespoon) grated ginger
15ml (1 tablespoon) finely chopped spring
   onion
3 petals star anise
dry cornflour
50g (2 oz) Indian tea
50g (2 oz) brown sugar
50g (2 oz) rice
oil for deep frying

Clean, wash and score the fish on
both sides. Marinate with the salt, rice
wine, grated ginger, spring onions
and star anise for 30 minutes, then roll
in dry cornflour.

Heat the oil and deep-fry the fish
until golden brown. Lift out and drain.
Put the tea, sugar and rice in a baking
tin lined with tinfoil. Cover closely
with a lid and put into a pre-heated
oven (220°C/425°F/Gas 7) until it
starts to smoke. Then lay the fish on a
rack over the smoking mixture, cover
closely again and return to the oven.
Reduce the temperature to 180°C/
350°F/Gas 4 and smoke for 10
minutes. Serve hot or cold.
Note: smoked fish can be prepared in
advance and then steamed to re-heat.
Serve sprinkled with sesame oil.

Stuffed Green Peppers

蝦苹釀青椒

300g (10 oz) shelled raw prawns
1 egg white
2ml (½ teaspoon) black pepper
15ml (1 tablespoon) cornflour
5ml (1 teaspoon) sesame oil
5ml (1 teaspoon) salt
50g (2 oz) pork back fat
75g (3 oz) bamboo shoots
7 small green peppers
dry cornflour
45ml (3 tablespoons) oil

Mince the prawns and mix with the egg white, pepper, 15ml (1 tablespoon) cornflour, sesame oil and salt. Mince the pork fat and bamboo shoots and blend into the prawn mixture. Cut the peppers into halves and dust the insides with dry cornflour. Divide the prawn mixture between them and press in firmly. Heat the oil and put in the peppers, stuffed side down. After 1 minute turn over, add 150ml (¼ pint, ½ cup) water and cook until the pan is almost dry. Lift out and serve.

151

Crackling Rice with Seafood

双鲜焗巴

150g (5 oz) raw shelled prawns
½ egg white
2ml (½ teaspoon) salt
20ml (4 teaspoons) cornflour
150g (5 oz) cleaned squid (see page 23)
6 water chestnuts
1 spring onion
1 slice ginger
300ml (½ pint, 1¼ cups) stock
15ml (1 tablespoon) soy sauce
16 pieces of rice cake (see page 18)
oil for deep frying

Marinate the prawns with the egg white, salt and 10ml (2 teaspoons) cornflour. Score the squid sac and cut into 2cm (1-inch) pieces. Cut the water chestnuts into halves and the spring onion into 1cm (½-inch) lengths. Mix 10ml (2 teaspoons) cornflour with 15ml (1 tablespoon) water.

Deep-fry the prawns for 20 seconds, then drain. Blanch the squid in boiling water for 1 minute and drain. Heat 45ml (3 tablespoons) oil and stir-fry the onion and ginger. Add the water chestnuts, then the prawns. Pour in the stock and soy sauce and bring to the boil. Thicken with cornflour, and at the last minute add the squid. Heat the oil to very hot and deep-fry the rice cakes until just coloured. Lift out, place on a deep serving plate and immediately pour the boiling sauce and seafood over the rice cakes. Serve at once.

Stir-fried Prawns with Spring Onions

葱油炰虾

450g (1 lb) cooked prawns with shells
3 spring onions
2 slices ginger
5ml (1 teaspoon) salt
15ml (1 tablespoon) rice wine
60ml (4 tablespoons) oil

Rinse the prawns and drain well. Cut the spring onions into 2cm (1-inch) lengths.

Heat the oil and stir-fry the onions and ginger. Add the prawns and stir-fry ove a high heat. Add the salt and rice wine and serve.

Stir-fried Mussels and Squid

淡菜
豆乾

20 frozen mussels
15ml (1 tablespoon) rice wine
1 small dried squid
1 spring onion
1 slice ginger
2ml (½ teaspoon) salt
15ml (1 tablespoon) soy sauce
10ml (2 teaspoons) sugar
45ml (3 tablespoons) oil

Marinate the mussels in the rice wine. Prepare the dried squid (see page 23), then score and cut into 5cm (2-inch) lengths.

Heat the oil and stir-fry the onions and ginger for 15 seconds. Add the mussels, then the dried squid. Season with salt, soy sauce and sugar and add 150ml (¼ pint, ⅔ cup) water. Boil until the pan is almost dry. Serve.

154

Braised Fish

红烧嘉腊鱼

1 small wrasse or carp
5ml (1 teaspoon) salt
15ml (1 tablespoon) rice wine
30ml (2 tablespoons) soy sauce
10g (½ oz) lily buds
3 pieces wood ears
1 spring onion
45ml (3 tablespoons) oil
2 slices ginger
25g (1 oz) green beans

Clean, wash and score the fish on both sides. Marinate with the salt, rice wine and soy sauce. Soak the lily buds in hot water for 30 minutes. Soak the wood ears in hot water for 30 minutes, then rinse well and cut into slices. Cut the spring onion into 1cm (½-inch) lengths.

Heat the oil and stir-fry the onions and ginger. Add the fish and fry until the skin is lightly browned. Then add the remaining marinade and 425ml (¾ pint, 1¾ cups) water, the lily buds, wood ears and green beans. Simmer until the fish is cooked (allow about 10 minutes for each 2cm/1 inch of fish thickness from the bottom of the pan). Serve with the vegetables on top and the sauce poured over.

Stir-fried Prawns with Cucumber

小蝦燶黄瓜

200g (7 oz) cooked prawns in
    their shells
1 cucumber
2 spring onions
6 slices ginger
45ml (3 tablespoons) oil
25ml (1½ tablespoons) rice
    wine
5ml (1 teaspoon) salt
black pepper

Rinse the prawns and drain well. Wash and cut the
cucumber into wedge-shaped pieces. Cut the spring onions
into 1cm (½-inch) lengths.
   Heat the oil and stir-fry the spring onions and ginger. Add
the cucumber, then the prawns. Season with the rice wine,
salt and a little black pepper. Serve at once.

Sweet and Sour Squid

糖醋小卷

300g (10 oz) squid
30ml (2 tablespoons) rice
    vinegar
25ml (1½ tablespoons) sugar
15ml (1 tablespoon) soy sauce
2ml (½ teaspoon) salt
15ml (1 tablespoon) rice wine
2 spring onions
7.5ml (1½ teaspoons) cornflour
3 slices ginger
25ml (1½ tablespoons) oil

Clean the squid according to directions on page 23. Keep
the body sacs whole. Mix the vinegar, sugar, soy sauce, salt
and rice wine with 60ml (4 tablespoons) water. Cut the
spring onions into 1cm (½-inch) lengths. Mix the cornflour
with 15ml (1 tablespoon) water.
   Blanch the squid in boiling water for 1 minute, then drain.
Heat the oil and stir-fry the ginger and onion. Pour in the
sauce, then add the squid. Stir well to coat in the sauce, then
mix in the cornflour paste. Serve.

Dish of Fortune

發財
有餘

1 small dried squid (see page 23)
10 small dried mushrooms
7g (¼ oz) 'black hair' fungus
150g (5 oz) fresh squid sac
75g (3 oz) bamboo shoots
10ml (2 teaspoons) cornflour
25g (1 oz) skinned broad beans
30ml (2 tablespoons) oil
salt and soy sauce to taste

Score the prepared dried squid in a criss-cross pattern on its lighter side and cut into 4cm (1½-inch) pieces. Soak the dried mushrooms in 275ml (½ pint, 1¼ cups) water for 1 hour. Then reserve the soaking water and discard the hard stalks. Soak the 'black hair' in very hot water for 3 minutes. Score the fresh squid on the outside and cut into 4cm (1½-inch) pieces. Slice the bamboo shoots. Mix the cornflour with 15ml (1 tablespoon) water.

Heat the oil and stir-fry the mushrooms. Add the bamboo shoots and the beans. Pour in the reserved mushroom water and bring to the boil. Add the squid and simmer for 3 minutes. Then season the gravy with salt and soy sauce. Thicken with cornflour and serve with the black hair laid on top of the dish.

158

Sea-fresh Greens

干貝芥菜胆

500g (1 lb) Chinese greens (gailan, choisam or
   bok choi)
25g (1 oz) dried shrimps
2 spring onions
10ml (2 teaspoons) cornflour
30ml (2 tablespoons) oil
300ml (½ pint, 1¾ cups) chicken stock
5ml (1 teaspoon) rice wine
pepper and salt
5ml (1 teaspoon) sesame oil

Wash and trim the Chinese greens. Put the dried shrimps into a pan of hot water and
bring to the boil. Boil for 2 minutes, then leave to soak for 15 minutes in the water.
Rinse well. Cut the spring onions into 1cm (½-inch) lengths. Mix the cornflour with
15ml (1 tablespoon) water.
   Boil the Chinese greens in the stock until tender. Meanwhile stir-fry the onions and
shrimps in the oil for 30 seconds. Lift out the greens on to a serving plate. Add the
onions and shrimps to the stock. Adjust the seasoning to taste and thicken with the
cornflour paste. Pour over the greens and serve.

Braised Sea Cucumbers with Ham

4 dried sea cucumbers (for
   preparation see page 18)
200g (7 oz) raw ham
200g (7 oz) bamboo shoots
5ml (1 teaspoon) cornflour
2 spring onions
15ml (1 tablespoon) lard
3 slices ginger
300ml (½ pint, 1¼ cups) stock
15ml (1 tablespoon) rice wine
15ml (1 tablespoon) soy sauce

Boil the prepared sea cucumbers for 45 minutes in water (or stock). Meanwhile cut the ham and bamboo into slices. Mix the cornflour with 15ml (1 tablespoon) water. Cut the spring onion into 1cm (½-inch) lengths.

Melt the lard and stir-fry the onion and ginger. Then add the stock and rice wine. When it boils add the sea cucumbers and soy sauce. Simmer for 45 minutes, add a little water if necessary and then add the ham and bamboo shoots. Simmer for another 10 minutes. Check the seasoning and thicken the sauce with the cornflour paste. Serve.

Stir-fried Squid with Coriander and Garlic

1 dried squid (for preparation
   see page 23)
5ml (1 teaspoon) salt
30ml (2 tablespoons) rice wine
20ml (4 teaspoons) cornflour
10 water chestnuts
50g (2 oz) coriander
3 cloves garlic
1 spring onion
30ml (2 tablespoons) oil
10ml (2 teaspoons) rice vinegar
salt and pepper

Score the prepared squid as shown on page 23, and cut into 4cm (1½-inch) squares. Marinate with the salt, 10ml (2 teaspoons) rice wine and 10ml (2 teaspoons) cornflour. Cut the water chestnuts into slices and chop the coriander finely. Chop the garlic and spring onion. Mix 10ml (2 teaspoons) cornflour with 15ml (1 tablespoon) water.

Drop the squid into boiling water and boil for 4 minutes. Lift out and drain. Heat the oil and stir-fry the garlic and onion. Add the water chestnuts and the squid. Pour in 110ml (⅕ pint, ½ cup) water and 20ml (4 teaspoons) rice wine and bring to the boil. Stir in the coriander and thicken with cornflour. Add the vinegar and season to taste. Serve.

Crab Omelette

2 small dressed crabs
30ml (2 tablespoons) soy sauce
15ml (1 tablespoon) rice wine
2 spring onions
15g (½ oz) ginger
4 eggs
45ml (3 tablespoons) oil

Remove all the meat from the crabs. Wash and reserve the shells. Marinate the crab meat in 15ml (1 tablespoon) soy sauce and the rice wine. Finely chop the spring onion and grate the ginger. Mix with the crab meat. Beat the eggs.

Heat the oil and stir-fry the crab. Add 15ml (1 tablespoon) soy sauce, then pour in the eggs. Stir gently until the egg is set, then serve garnished with the crab shells.

Quail Eggs with Ham and Shrimps

口進斗金

25g (1 oz) dried shrimps
45ml (3 tablespoons) rice wine
50g (2 oz) raw ham
12 quail eggs
25g (1 oz) broad beans
25ml (1½ tablespoons) oil
15ml (1 tablespoon) soy sauce
lettuce leaves

Put the dried shrimps into hot water and bring to the boil. Boil for 2 minutes, then leave to soak for 15 minutes before draining and mixing with the rice wine. Dice the ham. Hard-boil the quail eggs. Boil and skin the broad beans.

Heat the oil and stir-fry the shrimps. Reserve the rice wine marinade. Add the ham, then the quail eggs and broad beans. Season with the soy sauce and reserved rice wine. Serve on a plate garnished with lettuce leaves.

Note: the quail eggs may also be served in empty crab or scallop shells.

163

Seaweed Salad

蝦米海帶絲

25g (1 oz) dried kelp
10g (½ oz) dried shrimps
2 chillis
6 slices ginger
30ml (2 tablespoons) sesame oil
15ml (1 tablespoon) soy sauce

Boil the kelp in water for 10 minutes, then wash thoroughly in cold water. Cut into thin strips. Put the dried shrimps into hot water and boil for 3 minutes, then leave to soak for 15 minutes. De-seed and shred the chillis. Shred the ginger.

Heat the sesame oil and stir-fry the shrimps and ginger. Add the chillis, then the soy sauce. Arrange the kelp on a plate and lay the stir-fried chillis and shrimps on top. Mix well before serving.

Three-shreds Salad

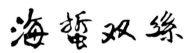

1 sheet jellyfish (for preparation see page 17)
2 small turnips
2 small carrots
2ml (½ teaspoon) salt
15ml (1 tablespoon) sesame oil
15ml (1 tablespoon) soy sauce
5ml (1 teaspoon) rice vinegar
5ml (1 teaspoon) sugar

Prepare and cut the jellyfish into very thin strips. Peel and shred the turnips and carrots. Mix with the salt and leave for 2 hours. Then rinse and squeeze dry between the hands. Arrange the jellyfish, turnip and carrot shreds on a plate and pour over the sesame oil, soy sauce, rice vinegar and sugar. Mix well before serving.

Braised Scallops and
Quail Eggs

干貝双球

24 quail eggs
6 frozen scallops
15ml (1 tablespoon) rice wine
300g (10 oz) carrot
10ml (2 teaspoons) cornflour
300ml (½ pint, 1¼ cups) good chicken
    stock
a few leaves of choisam

Hard-boil and shell the quail eggs.
De-frost the scallops and marinate in
the rice wine. Peel and boil the carrots
in lightly salted water. Then cut into
small balls. Mix the cornflour with
15ml (1 tablespoon) water.
   Steam the scallops in the marinade
for 10 minutes. Cool and cut into
shreds. Put the eggs, stock and carrot
balls into a pan and bring to the boil.
Add the scallop shreds and choisam,
then thicken with the cornflour paste
before serving.

166

Scallops and Baby Corn

干貝玉米筍

4 frozen scallops
15ml (1 tablespoon) rice wine
12 button mushrooms
45ml (3 tablespoons) oil
pinch of salt
300g (10 oz) canned baby corn
15ml (1 tablespoon) soy sauce

De-frost and marinate the scallops in the rice wine. Wipe and trim the mushrooms.
Steam the scallops in the rice wine for 10 minutes. Allow to cool, then cut into shreds. Heat the oil and stir-fry the mushrooms with a pinch of salt until soft. Then lift out and put on one side. Stir-fry the baby corn in the same oil. Add the soy sauce and a little water and bring to the boil. Return the mushrooms and simmer until almost dry. Serve with the scallop shreds scattered over the top.

Braised Eel

紅燒馬鞍橋

600g (1¼ lb) conger eel
45ml (3 tablespoons) soy sauce
25ml (1½ tablespoons)
    cornflour
75g (3 oz) lean pork
100g (4 oz) bamboo shoots
6 cloves garlic
10 spring onions
4 slices ginger
30ml (2 tablespoons) rice wine
15ml (1 tablespoon) sugar
10ml (2 teaspoons) vinegar
450ml (¾ pint, 2 cups) stock
5ml (1 teaspoon) sesame oil
salt and pepper
oil for deep frying

Skin and bone the eel and cut into 6cm (2½-inch) portions. Marinate with 15ml (1 tablespoon) soy sauce and 15ml (1 tablespoon) cornflour. Slice the pork and bamboo shoots. Mince the garlic. Mix 7.5ml (½ tablespoon) cornflour with 15ml (1 tablespoon) water.

Heat the oil and deep-fry the eel for 1 minute. Drain well. Put 30ml (2 tablespoons) oil in a pan and stir-fry the onions, ginger and garlic. Add the pork, eel, bamboo shoots, rice wine, 30ml (2 tablespoons) soy sauce, sugar, vinegar and the stock and simmer for 40 minutes. Season to taste and thicken with the cornflour paste. Serve sprinkled with sesame oil.

Tiger's Tail

搶虎尾

350g (12 oz) mackerel
10ml (2 teaspoons) finely
    chopped spring onion
10ml (2 teaspoons) grated
    ginger
20ml (4 teaspoons) Sichuan
    peppercorns
150ml (¼ pint, ⅔ cup) stock
5ml (1 teaspoon) rice wine
5ml (1 teaspoon) vinegar
2ml (½ teaspoon) black pepper
5 cloves garlic
15ml (1 tablespoon) sesame oil
15ml (1 tablespoon) oil
coriander leaves

Clean, wash and fillet the mackerel. Cut into thin, finger-long slices. Marinate with the onions, ginger, 10ml (2 teaspoons) Sichuan peppercorns and 30ml (2 tablespoons) of the stock. Mix the remaining stock with the rice wine, vinegar and black pepper. Chop the garlic finely.

Steam the fish in its marinade for 6 minutes, then discard the onions, ginger and Sichuan pepper. Boil the prepared stock and pour it over the mackerel. Sprinkle the garlic on top. Heat the sesame oil and cooking oil with 10ml (2 teaspoons) Sichuan peppercorns and pour over the garlic. Garnish with coriander leves before serving.

Stir-fried Dried Squid

鹽爆魷魚

2 dried squid (for preparation see page 23)
2 spring onions
2 chillis
30ml (2 tablespoons) oil
2 slices ginger
2ml (½ teaspoon) salt
15ml (1 tablespoon) rice wine
15ml (1 tablespoon) chopped coriander
5ml (1 teaspoon) sesame oil

Score the prepared squid cross-wise on the lighter sides and cut into 5cm (2-inch) squares. Cut the spring onions and de-seeded chillis into fine shreds.

Put the squid into boiling water and blanch for about 4 minutes. Drain well. Heat the oil and stir-fry the onion, chillis and ginger. Add the squid and stir-fry with a little salt. Season with rice wine and mix in the coriander. Serve sprinkled with sesame oil.

Family Reunion

全家福

2 eggs
25ml (1 ½ tablespoons) oil
300g (10 oz) pork paste (see page 26)
2 sheets nori seaweed
5ml (1 teaspoon) cornflour
300g (10 oz) chicken joints
6 spring onions
6 slices ginger
15ml (1 tablespoon) rice wine
500g (1 lb) Chinese cabbage
75g (3 oz) beansprouts
50g (2 oz) silk noodles
150g (5 oz) cooked ham, or Chinese roast
    pork
1 litre (2 pints, 5 cups) boiling stock
8 fish balls
25g (1 oz) peas
soy sauce, salt and pepper

Beat the eggs and fry in the oil to make 2 small pancakes. Turn out on a flat surface and leave to cool. Then spread a quarter of the pork paste over each, cover with a sheet of *nori* and roll up tightly into a cigar shape. Steam for 20 minutes. Cool and slice. Shape the remaining pork paste with a little soy sauce and cornflour into walnut-sized balls and steam for 25 minutes. Marinate the chicken with 2 onions, 2 slices ginger and the rice wine, then steam for 20 minutes. Cut into bite-sized pieces. Wash and tear the Chinese cabbage into pieces. Wash and trim the beansprouts. Blanch in boiling water.

Cut the silk noodles into 13cm (5-inch) lengths and soak until soft. Cut the ham into bite-sized pieces. Arrange the Chinese cabbage in the bottom of a large casserole. Put the chicken, onions, ginger and ham on top. Then add the meatballs, fish balls, silk noodles, peas and sliced egg rolls. Pour over the boiling stock and simmer for 15 minutes. Season to taste and add the blanched beansprouts before serving.

Gold and Silver Broth

蓬蒿
金銀羹

75g (3 oz) pig's liver
10ml (2 teaspoons) rice wine
5ml (1 teaspoon) grated ginger
2 squares beancurd
50g (2 oz) bamboo shoots
75g (3 oz) watercress
1 spring onion
600ml (1 pint, 2½ cups) good stock
salt and pepper to taste
15ml (1 tablespoon) cornflour

Cut the liver into thin slices and marinate in the rice wine and ginger. Cut the beancurd into 1cm (½-inch) cubes. Cut the bamboo shoots into similar-sized pieces. Wash the watercress and tear off the leaves, discarding the stalks. Chop the spring onion. Mix the cornflour with 30ml (2 tablespoons) water.

Bring the stock to the boil and add the spring onion, bamboo shoots and watercress. Season to taste. Slide in the beancurd, then the liver. Thicken with the cornflour paste and serve immediately.

174

Stuffed Omelettes

蝦肉蛋餃

180g (6 oz) minced pork
50g (2 oz) raw prawns, shelled and de-veined
20ml (4 teaspoons) rice wine
2ml (½ teaspoon) salt
5ml (1 teaspoon) soy sauce
10ml (2 teaspoons) cornflour
1 dried mushroom
3 large eggs
200ml (⅓ pint, 1 cup) stock
a few stalks of watercress and carrot shreds,
    blanched

Mix the pork with the chopped prawns, 10ml (2 teaspoons) rice wine, salt, soy sauce and cornflour. Beat the eggs and in an oiled frying-pan make tiny omelettes using only 15ml (1 tablespoon) egg at a time. Lay the finished omelettes on a flat surface and put a spoonful of the pork mixture on each. Fold in the sides and roll them up into neat packages. Put into a shallow bowl and pour over the stock. Add the dried mushroom, previously soaked and with the hard stalk removed. Steam for 15 minutes. Garnish with watercress and carrot shreds.

Three-colour Steamed Egg Cake

三色蛋糕

6 eggs
5ml (1 teaspoon) salt
15ml (1 tablespoon) rice wine
30ml (2 tablespoons) minced
    ham
15ml (1 tablespoon) peas
lard

Beat the eggs and add the salt, rice wine and ⅔ of the ham. Grease a loose-bottomed tin with the lard and pour in the egg mixture. Put into a steamer over a low heat. After 5 minutes add the peas and steam for another 10 minutes before sprinkling over the remaining ham shreds. Steam for another 5 minutes, then lift out and allow to cool. Cut into slices before serving.

Stuffed Eggs

肉圆镶蛋

6 hard-boiled eggs
200g (7 oz) minced pork
10ml (2 teaspoons) rice wine
10ml (2 teaspoons) soy sauce
10ml (2 teaspoons) cornflour
2ml (½ teaspoon) salt
finely chopped ham for garnish

Shell and cut the eggs into halves lengthwise. Take out the egg yolks, reserving three. Mix the minced pork with the rice wine, soy sauce, cornflour and salt, and beat in the reserved hard-boiled egg yolks. Fill the egg-white halves with the mixture, garnish with the ham and steam for 15 minutes.

177

Egg Fu Yung

三鲜炒蛋

6 eggs
2ml (½ teaspoon) salt
3 dried mushrooms
50g (2 oz) green beans
50g (2 oz) bamboo shoots
2 spring onions
15ml (1 tablespoon) oil
50g (2 oz) prawns
50g (2 oz) pork shreds
50g (2 oz) ham shreds
15ml (1 tablespoon) soy sauce

Beat the eggs with the salt. Soak the dried mushrooms in water until soft. Discard the hard stalks and slice the caps. Trim and slice the beans. Cut the bamboo shoots into shreds and chop the spring onions. Heat the oil and stir-fry the onions, then add the prawns, pork and ham shreds. Stir-fry for 1 minute, then add the mushrooms, beans and bamboo shoots and stir-fry for another minute. Season with soy sauce, then pour in the beaten egg and mix well. Leave to cook on a low heat until the egg starts to set, then finish under the grill. Turn out and serve.

Onion Flower Fried Eggs

葱花炒蛋

6 eggs
3 spring onions
2ml (½ teaspoon) salt
10ml (2 teaspoons) soy sauce
30ml (2 tablespoons) oil
several lettuce leaves

Beat the eggs with the salt and soy sauce. Finely chop the spring onions and mix into the eggs.

Heat the oil and pour in the eggs. Stir gently over a high heat until just set. Lift out and serve on a bed of lettuce leaves.

181

Pork and Salted Eggs

200g (7 oz) minced pork
5ml (1 teaspoon) rice wine
15ml (1 tablespoon) soy sauce
2ml (½ teaspoon) salt
3 fresh eggs
2 salted eggs
10ml (2 teaspoons) finely chopped spring
    onions

Mix the minced pork with the rice wine, soy sauce and salt. Beat the fresh eggs and mix into the pork mixture. Put into a serving bowl. Wash and break the salted eggs over the top of the pork and sprinkle with the chopped onions. Steam for 30 minutes.

Pan-sticky Beancurd

鍋貼豆腐

4 squares beancurd
150g (5 oz) prawns, minced
25g (1 oz) ham, minced
2 eggs
15ml (1 tablespoon) finely chopped onion
10ml (2 teaspoons) minced ginger
5ml (1 teaspoon) ground Sichuan pepper
15ml (1 tablespoon) rice wine
15ml (1 tablespoon) cornflour
2ml (½ teaspoon) salt
2 sheets dried beancurd skin
60ml (4 tablespoons) flour
75ml (5 tablespoons) cold water
oil for deep frying

Mash the beancurd and mix it with the minced prawns and ham. Beat in 1 egg, the onion, ginger, Sichuan pepper, rice wine, cornflour and salt. Dampen the beancurd skins and lay flat on a table. Spread the mashed beancurd over each sheet and fold up into two flat packets. Steam for 30 minutes and allow to cool. Mix a batter of the egg, flour and water and dip each packet in the batter before deep-frying in the hot oil. Serve cut into slices.

Hakka Beancurd

東江釀豆腐

50g (2 oz) raw shelled prawns	2 spring onions
50g (2 oz) minced pork	2 cloves garlic
5g (¼ oz) Sichuan preserved vegetable	6 squares beancurd
	300ml (½ pint, 1¼ cups) chicken stock
10ml (2 teaspoons) egg white	
15ml (1 tablespoon) cornflour	25ml (1½ tablespoons) soy sauce
5ml (1 teaspoon) rice wine	
2ml (½ teaspoon) sugar	oil for deep frying
pinch of salt	

Mince the prawns and mix into the pork with the finely chopped Sichuan preserved vegetable. Then beat in the egg white, 5ml (1 teaspoon) cornflour, rice wine, sugar and salt. Chop the spring onions finely and mix 5ml (1 teaspoon) into the meat paste. Crush the garlic and mix with the remaining onion. Mix 10ml (2 teaspoons) cornflour with 15ml (1 tablespoon) water. Cut the beancurd squares in halves and fry in moderately hot oil for about 5 minutes. Then drain and hollow out a small depression in the centre of each piece of beancurd. Fill with the meat paste and arrange the squares in a saucepan. Pour in the stock, soy sauce, remaining onion and garlic and simmer gently for 30 minutes. Lift out the beancurd and arrange on a serving plate; thicken the gravy and pour it over the beancurd. Serve.

Red-cooked Beancurd

紅燒炆豆腐

6 squares beancurd	1 clove garlic, crushed
50g (2 oz) bamboo shoots	10ml (2 teaspoons) cornflour
50g (2 oz) snow peas	10ml (2 teaspoons) soy sauce
50g (2 oz) fresh mushrooms	10ml (2 teaspoons) sugar
75g (3 oz) Cantonese roast pork	300ml (½ pint, 1¼ cups) stock
1 chilli	oil for deep frying
2 spring onions	

Cut the beancurd squares into three. Slice the bamboo shoots, trim the snow peas and wipe and slice the mushrooms. Cut the pork into thin slices. De-seed and chop the chilli. Cut the spring onions into 1cm (½-inch) lengths. Mix the cornflour with 15ml (1 tablespoon) water.

Heat the oil and deep-fry the beancurd over a moderate heat until brown. Lift out and drain. Heat a pan with 15ml (1 tablespoon) oil and stir-fry the chilli, onion and garlic. Then add the vegetables and pork. Season with soy and sugar and pour in the stock. Simmer for 10 minutes, then slide in the beancurd. Check the seasoning, thicken the gravy and serve.

185

Palace Beancurd

天厨
老豆腐

10 squares beancurd
1 small boiling fowl
2 slices ginger
2 spring onions
2 petals star anise
5ml (1 teaspoon) Sichuan peppercorns
5ml (1 teaspoon) salt
14 dried mushrooms
150g (5 oz) ham
1 can abalone
150g scallops
10ml (2 teaspoons) cornflour

Put the beancurd into boiling water and simmer for 3 hours, then drain and cut each square into 4 triangles. Put the chicken into a pan with sufficient water to cover and add the ginger, onions, star anise, Sichuan peppercorns and salt. Simmer for 3 hours. Meanwhile soak the dried mushrooms for 30 minutes, then discard the hard stalks. Mix the cornflour with 15ml (1 tablespoon) water. Slice the ham, abalone and scallops. When the chicken has finished cooking, strain the stock and put it into a clean pan with the beancurd and scallops. Simmer until all the stock has gone, taking care it does not burn. Arrange the mushrooms, ham, and abalone round a pudding bowl and put the beancurd and scallops in the middle. Cover with tinfoil and steam for 2 hours. Then drain off the juice and turn out upside down on to a plate. Boil the juice, adjust the seasoning and thicken with the cornflour paste. Pour over and serve.

186

Mashed Beancurd

三色豆腐泥

5 dried mushrooms
25g (1 oz) peas
4 beancurd squares
50g (2 oz) silk or pea-starch noodles
2 spring onions
10 cooked prawns
1 slice ginger
100g (4 oz) minced pork
60ml (4 tablespoons) oil

Soak the dried mushrooms for 30 minutes, then discard the hard stalk and chop the caps finely. Boil the peas in lightly salted water until soft, then drain. Chop the beancurd into small dice. Soak the noodles in warm water to soften, then chop into ½cm (¼-inch) pieces. Chop the spring onions finely.

Heat 15ml (1 tablespoon) oil and stir-fry the mushrooms for a minute. Then lift out and in the same oil stir-fry the prawns and ginger for a minute. Lift out and reserve. Clean the pan and heat 45ml (3 tablespoons) oil. Stir-fry the pork, then add the beancurd and silk noodles. Mash the beancurd while stir-frying it and add a pinch of salt, half the mushrooms and the spring onions. Turn into a bowl and beat the mixture well before pressing it down firmly. Turn out upside down on to a plate and garnish with the prawns, peas and reserved mushrooms.

Mapo's Beancurd

麻婆豆腐

6 squares beancurd
7.5ml (1½ teaspoons) cornflour
15ml (1 tablespoon) chilli-bean
　　sauce
15ml (1 tablespoon) finely
　　chopped spring onion
15ml (1 tablespoon) finely
　　chopped ginger
2 cloves garlic, crushed
100g (4 oz) minced pork
15ml (1 tablespoon) rice wine
25ml (1½ tablespoons) soy
　　sauce
150ml (¼ pint, ⅔ cup) stock
30ml (2 tablespoons) oil

Cut the beancurd into 1cm (½-inch) cubes. Mix the cornflour with 15ml (1 tablespoon) water.

Heat the oil and stir-fry the onion, ginger and garlic. Then add the pork and stir-fry for 1 minute before adding the chilli-bean sauce. Pour in the rice wine, soy sauce and stock and bring to the boil. Slide in the beancurd and simmer for 5 minutes. Thicken with the cornflour and serve.

Family Beancurd

6 squares beancurd
25g (1 oz) spring onions
15ml (1 tablespoon) minced
　　ginger
10ml (2 teaspoons) crushed
　　garlic
5ml (1 teaspoon) chilli-bean
　　sauce
10ml (2 teaspoons) soy sauce
10ml (2 teaspoons) sugar
10ml (2 teaspoons) rice wine
150ml (¼ pint, ⅔ cup) stock
5ml (1 teaspoon) sesame oil
oil for deep frying

Cut each beancurd square into 4 triangles. Cut the spring onions into 5cm (2-inch) lengths.

Heat the oil to moderately hot and deep-fry the beancurd triangles for 4 minutes. Lift out and drain. Heat 30ml (2 tablespoons) oil in a pan and stir-fry the ginger and garlic. Add the chilli-bean sauce, then the soy sauce, sugar, rice wine and stock. Bring to the boil and add the beancurd. Simmer for 5 minutes, then serve sprinkled with sesame oil.

Stir-fried Dried Mushrooms with Chinese Greens

双菇菜心

6 large dried mushrooms
6 'oyster' mushrooms
500g (1 lb) Chinese greens (gailan,
    choisam or bok choi)
15ml (1 tablespoon) soy sauce
salt
60ml (4 tablespoons) oil

Soak the dried mushrooms for 30 minutes, then discard the hard caps. Wipe and trim the stalk ends of the oyster mushrooms. Slice into halves. Wash and trim the Chinese greens.

Heat a pan with 30ml (2 tablespoons) oil and stir-fry the oyster mushrooms. Then add the dried mushrooms and 7.5ml (½ tablespoon) soy sauce. Stir-fry for a few moments and put on one side. Heat another pan with 30ml (2 tablespoons) oil and stir-fry the Chinese greens with a pinch of salt. Add 10ml (2 teaspoons) soy sauce and about 150ml (¼ pint, ⅔ cup) water and simmer until the greens are cooked. Drain and arrange on a plate. Then add the two kinds of mushrooms and serve.

190

Frozen Beancurd

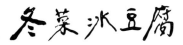

3 squares beancurd
10 button mushrooms
1 small cauliflower
2 spring onions
30ml (2 tablespoons) Tianjin cabbage
10ml (2 teaspoons) soy sauce
salt
45ml (3 tablespoons) oil

Put the beancurd squares in the freezer (or ice-making compartment of the refrigerator) overnight. Then thaw in warm water, squeeze dry and cut each square into 4 slices. Wipe and trim the stalk ends of the mushrooms. Wash and cut the cauliflower into florets. Finely chop the spring onions.

Boil the cauliflower florets in lightly salted water for 5 minutes, then drain. Heat the oil and stir-fry the mushrooms with a pinch of salt until soft. Lift out the mushrooms and put the beancurd into the mushroom oil. Stir-fry for a moment, then add the soy sauce and 425ml (¾ pint, 2 cups) water. Bring to the boil and add the Tianjin cabbage and the mushrooms. Boil gently until the pan is almost dry and mix in the cauliflower. Adjust the seasoning and scatter over the chopped spring onions before serving.

Aubergine with 'Fish-fragrant' Sauce

魚香茄子

500g (1 lb) aubergines
10ml (2 teaspoons) cornflour
6 spring onions
15g (½ oz) ginger
3 cloves garlic
10ml (2 teaspoons) chilli-bean
    sauce
30ml (2 tablespoons) soy sauce
15ml (1 tablespoon) sugar
150ml (¼ pint, ⅔ cup) stock
15ml (1 tablespoon) rice
    vinegar
oil for deep frying
5ml (1 teaspoon) sesame oil

Wash and cut the aubergines into 5cm (2-inch) strips. Mix the cornflour with 15ml (1 tablespoon) water. Finely chop the spring onions, ginger and garlic.

Heat the oil and deep-fry the aubergine for 3 minutes over a low heat. Drain well. Heat a pan with 15ml (1 tablespoon) oil and stir-fry the onions, ginger, garlic and chilli-bean sauce. Then add the soy sauce, sugar and stock. Put in the aubergines and bring to the boil. Boil for about 2 minutes, then mix in the vinegar. Check the seasoning and serve with the sesame oil sprinkled over.

Dry-fried French Beans

乾燸四季豆

500g (1 lb) french beans
30ml (2 tablespoons) dried
    shrimps
30ml (2 tablespoons) Sichuan
    preserved vegetable
75g (3 oz) minced pork
3 spring onions
4 slices ginger
20ml (4 teaspoons) soy sauce
10ml (2 teaspoons) vinegar
5ml (1 teaspoon) sugar
5ml (1 teaspoon) sesame oil
oil for deep frying

String the beans and cut them into 5cm (2-inch) lengths. Soak the dried shrimps in hot water for 30 minutes, then rinse well. Chop the Sichuan vegetable and the spring onions finely. Deep-fry the beans until they are wrinkled, then drain well. Heat 15ml (1 tablespoon) oil and stir-fry the spring onions and ginger, then add the pork, shrimps and Sichuan vegetable and continue stir-frying for another minute. Add the beans, then the soy sauce, vinegar and sugar. Mix well and serve sprinkled with sesame oil.

193

Four-jewelled Plate

1 can baby corn
10 dried mushrooms
4 carrots
1kg (2 lb) Chinese greens (gailan, choisam or bok choi)
10ml (2 teaspoons) cornflour
10ml (2 teaspoons) soy sauce
salt and pepper to taste

Drain the baby corn and cut each cob in half lengthwise. Soak the dried mushrooms for 1 hour, then reserve their soaking water and discard the hard stalks. Peel the carrots and carve a design on two sides. Slice the carrots lengthwise. Wash and trim the Chinese greens. Mix the cornflour with 15ml (1 tablespoon) water. Blanch all the vegetables separately in boiling water, then arrange in a deep plate. Put the mushrooms in first, then the carrots, baby corn and the Chinese greens on top. Steam for 30 minutes. Drain out the liquid into a pan and add the reserved mushroom water and soy sauce. Bring to the boil and season to taste before thickening with the cornflour. Turn the vegetables out upside-down without breaking the arrangement and pour over the gravy before serving.

Steamed Winter Melon Soup

錦繡
冬瓜盅

2.5kg (5 lb) winter melon (or the end of a
  big marrow)
4 dried mushrooms
125g (4 oz) cooked pork (Cantonese roast
  pork)
150g (5 oz) chicken, without bones
125g (4 oz) shelled prawns
50g (2 oz) ham
2 chicken livers
2 chicken gizzards
100g (3½ oz) bamboo shoots
4 slices ginger
15ml (1 tablespoon) rice wine
900ml (1½ pints, 3½ cups) stock

Wash and de-seed the melon. (If
desired cut the top edge in a zig-zag
and carve a design in the skin.) Put the
melon in a bowl. Soak the
mushrooms in warm water for 30
minutes, then discard the stalks and
dice the caps. Cut the meats into 1cm
(½-inch) pieces. Dice the bamboo
shoots into 1cm (½-inch) cubes.
Blanch all the uncooked meats in
boiling water, then drain before put-
ting them into the melon. Add the
bamboo shoots and mushrooms
together with the ginger and rice
wine. Heat the stock to boiling and
pour in sufficient to reach 4cm (1½
inches) below the top of the melon.
Steam for 40 minutes; check the
seasoning and serve hot.

195

Stir-fried Bamboo Shoots with Red-in-snow

笋丝煨胡蘿

180g (6 oz) bamboo shoots
75g (3 oz) carrot
100g (3½ oz) canned red-in-snow
30ml (2 tablespoons) oil
5ml (1 teaspoon) light soy sauce

Cut the bamboo shoots and the carrot into matchstick shreds. Soak the red-in-snow in water for 4 minutes. Then drain and cut into 1cm (½-inch) lengths. Heat the oil and stir-fry the bamboo for 30 seconds. Add the carrot and red-in-snow and continue stir-frying for another minute. Season with soy sauce and serve.

Arhat's Fast

素什錦

5 dried mushrooms
3 wood ears
250g (8 oz) broccoli
50g (2 oz) carrot
4 water chestnuts
75g (3 oz) bamboo shoots
25g (1 oz) skinned broad beans
1 can lotus root
6 fried beancurd squares
30ml (2 tablespoons) oil
300ml (½ pint, 1¼ cups) vegetarian stock
15ml (1 tablespoon) light soy sauce
5ml (1 teaspoon) sesame oil

Soak the dried mushrooms and the wood ears separately for 30 minutes. Then discard the hard mushroom stalks, rinse and slice the wood ears. Wash and tear the broccoli into florets. Cut the carrot into thin slices and the water chestnuts into halves. Slice the bamboo shoots and the canned lotus root. Cut the beancurd squares into quarters.

Heat the oil and stir-fry the mushrooms and wood ears. Add the bamboo shoots, carrots and lotus root. Pour in the stock and soy sauce and bring to the boil. Add the water chestnuts, broccoli, beancurd and beans and boil until the broccoli is cooked. Lift out the vegetables and serve sprinkled with sesame oil.

Stir-fried Red and Green peppers

鱼香双椒

100g (4 oz) minced pork
10ml (2 teaspoons) soy sauce
5ml (1 teaspoon) cornflour
5ml (1 teaspoon) rice wine
pinch of salt
300g (10 oz) green peppers
2 fresh chillis
30ml (2 tablespoon) sugar
2 cloves garlic
2 spring onions
3 slices ginger
45ml (3 tablespoons) oil

Marinate the minced pork with the soy sauce, cornflour, rice wine and salt. De-seed the peppers and chillis; cut the peppers into bite-sized pieces and the chillis into thin shreds. Mix the sweet bean sauce with the sugar and 30ml (2 tablespoons) water. Finely chop the spring onions, ginger and garlic. Heat the oil and stir-fry the green peppers. Then lift them out and stir-fry the chillis for about 15 seconds. Lift the chillis out and put in the meat. Add more oil if necessary and stir-fry until the meat separates. Add the ginger, onions and garlic, then return the green peppers to the pan. Finally, stir in the sweet bean paste and chillis and mix well. Serve.

Cabbage Rolls

奶油
菜捲

1 cabbage
2 dried mushrooms
50g (2 oz) shelled prawns
25ml (1½ tablespoons) rice wine
2 chicken livers
150g (5 oz) pork
5 snow peas
50g (2 oz) cooked ham
15ml (1 tablespoon) flour
150ml (¼ pint, ⅔ cup) stock
15ml (1 tablespoon) milk
45ml (3 tablespoons) oil

Select eight good cabbage leaves and blanch in boiling water. Soak the dried mushrooms in water for 30 minutes, then shred the caps. Marinate the prawns in 7.5ml (1½ teaspoons) rice wine. Blanch the livers in boiling water and then shred. Cut the pork into matchstick shreds. Shred the snow peas and ham.

Heat 30ml (2 tablespoons) oil in a pan and stir-fry the pork shreds. Add the mushrooms, prawns, livers, snow peas and ham and mix well together. Put on one side. Lay flat the cabbage leaves and use the stir-fried mixture to make a filling for each leaf. Fold in the sides and roll up the leaves into small packets. Lay on a plate and steam for 30 minutes. Meanwhile heat 15ml (1 tablespoon) oil and stir-fry the flour. Then pour in the stock, milk and remaining rice wine. Stir very well and bring to the boil. Simmer for a few minutes, then pour over the cabbage rolls before serving.

Red-in-snow with Mushrooms

菌油炒雪筍

100g (4 oz) canned red-in-snow
250g (8 oz) bamboo shoots
100g (4 oz) fresh mushrooms
10ml (2 teaspoons) cornflour
15ml (1 tablespoon) soy sauce
150ml (¼ pint, ⅔ cup) good
    stock
45ml (3 tablespoons) oil

Soak the red-in-snow for 4 minutes in cold water, then drain
well and cut into 1cm (½-inch) lengths. Slice the bamboo
shoots. Wipe and slice the mushrooms. Mix the cornflour
with 15ml (1 tablespoon) water.

Heat the oil and stir-fry the mushrooms until soft. Lift out
and reserve the mushrooms, leaving the oil in the pan.
Stir-fry the bamboo shoots in this oil, then add the
red-in-snow and finally return the mushrooms to the pan.
Add the soy sauce and the stock and bring to the boil. Then
thicken with the cornflour paste and serve.

Sweet and Sour Vegetables

糖醋素三片

4 dried mushrooms
1 carrot
100g (4 oz) water chestnuts
3 sticks celery
10ml (2 teaspoons) cornflour
5ml (1 teaspoon) salt
15ml (1 tablespoon) sugar
15ml (1 tablespoon) rice
    vinegar
15ml (1 tablespoon) soy sauce
2ml (½ teaspoon) sesame oil
30ml (2 tablespoons) oil

Soak the mushrooms in 150ml (¼ pint, ⅔ cup) warm water
for 1 hour. Reserve the soaking water, discard the stalks and
finely chop the caps. Peel and slice the carrot. Cut the water
chestnuts into thin slices. Wash and cut the celery into 2cm
(1-inch) angled slices. Mix the cornflour with 15ml (1
tablespoon) water.

Heat the oil and stir-fry the mushrooms. Then add the
carrot, water chestnuts and celery together with the salt.
Pour in the mushroom water, sugar, vinegar and soy sauce
and bring to the boil. Boil for about 4 minutes, then thicken
with the cornflour paste. Serve sprinkled with sesame oil.

Frozen Beancurd and Mushrooms

双冬烤麩

4 squares beancurd
4 dried mushrooms
75g (3 oz) bamboo shoots
a pinch of salt
15ml (1 tablespoon) soy sauce
15ml (1 tablespoon) sugar
5ml (1 teaspoon) sesame oil
45ml (3 tablespoons) oil

Put the beancurd in the freezer or the freezing compartment of the refrigerator overnight. Then de-frost in a bowl of warm water. Squeeze dry and cut each square into four. Soak the dried mushrooms in warm water for 30 minutes, then discard the stalks and cut the caps into quarters. Slice the bamboo shoots.

Heat the oil and stir-fry the mushrooms. Then put in the beancurd and the bamboo shoots. Season with a pinch of salt and add a little water. Bring to the boil and add the soy sauce and sugar. Simmer until the pan is almost dry and then serve sprinkled with the sesame oil.

Sweet and Sour Youtiao

素排骨

3 youtiao (deep-fried batter sticks)
100g (4 oz) red-bean paste
30ml (2 tablespoons) sugar
30ml (2 tablespoons) vinegar
10ml (2 teaspoons) cornflour
2 spring onions, very finely chopped
oil for deep frying

Cut the *youtiao* into 5cm (2-inch) lengths and stuff each piece with a little red-bean paste. Mix the sugar, vinegar and cornflour with 150ml (¼ pint, ⅔ cup) water.

Heat the oil to very hot and fry the *youtiao* until crisp and brown. Lift out and drain. Heat 15ml (1 tablespoon) oil in a pan and add the vinegar sauce. Bring to the boil and pour over the *youtiao*. Serve garnished with finely chopped onion.

Lohan's Delight

罪 漢 齋

6 baby corn shoots
6 sticks asparagus
½ cucumber
4 large dried mushrooms
10 canned straw mushrooms
2 carrots
75g (3 oz) bamboo shoots
250g (8 oz) choisam
15ml (1 tablespoon) cornflour
1 can gingko nuts
7g (¼ oz) 'black hair' fungus
300ml (½ pint, 1¼ cups) good stock
10ml (2 teaspoons) rice wine
5ml (1 teaspoon) sugar
10ml (2 teaspoons) soy sauce
5ml (1 teaspoon) sesame oil

Cut the corn stalks in half lenghwise. Trim the asparagus. Cut the cucumber into 8cm (3-inch) batons. Soak the dried mushrooms, then discard the stalks and slice the caps. Peel and cut the carrot into long, thin slices, and the bamboo into similar-sized slices. Wash and cut the *choisam* into 10cm (4-inch) lengths. Mix the cornflour with 30ml (2 tablespoons) water. Soak the 'black hair' fungus for 30 minutes in warm water. Boil some lightly salted water and blanch the corn shoots. Then drain and arrange on a warmed serving dish. Next, cook the carrot until soft, then drain and arrange on the plate. At the same time bring the stock to the boil and add the asparagus. Cook until tender, then arrange on the plate. Cook the bamboo shoots in fresh boiling water. Put the mushrooms into the stock, then the *choisam*. Cook the cucumber (after the bamboo shoots) in the water. When all the vegetables are cooked, blanch the 'black hair' in the stock and arrange on top of the dish. Season the stock with rice wine, sugar and soy sauce. Thicken with the cornflour paste and pour it over the arranged vegetables. Sprinkle sesame oil over the dish before serving.

Stir-fried Mushrooms with Chinese Greens

蔴菇塌稞菜

10 button mushrooms
500g (1 lb) Chinese greens (choisam, gailan or bok choi)
50g (2 oz) bean sprouts
60ml (4 tablespoons) oil
5ml (1 teaspoon) salt
15ml (1 tablespoon) soy sauce
10ml (2 teaspoons) sugar

Wipe and trim the mushrooms. Wash and trim the Chinese greens. Pick over the bean sprouts and blanch in boiling water.

Heat the oil and stir-fry the mushrooms. When soft, lift out and reserve. Put the Chinese greens into the pan with the salt and stir-fry for a few moments. Add the soy sauce, sugar and some water and boil until the cabbage is cooked. Return the mushrooms to the pan, mix well and serve garnished with the bean sprouts.

Celery Salad

梨山芹菜

250g (8 oz) celery
10ml (2 teaspoons) sugar
15ml (1 tablespoon) vinegar
2ml (½ teaspoon) salt
5ml (1 teaspoon) Sichuan peppercorns
100ml (3½ fl oz, ½ cup) sesame oil
15ml (1 tablespoon) made English mustard

Trim and wash the celery and cut into 5cm (2-inch) lengths. Split any big stalks in half lengthwise. Blanch in boiling water, then refresh in cold water before draining and tossing in the sugar, vinegar and salt. Leave for 1 hour.

Heat a pan with the sesame oil and Sichuan peppercorns over a low heat for 3 minutes. Then strain out the peppercorns and allow the oil to cool before mixing with the mustard. Just before serving drain the celery and toss in the flavoured oil.

Sichuan Pickles

什錦泡菜

selection of broccoli, cauliflower, carrot,
    red radishes, string beans, snow peas,
    white radish, cucumber, Chinese
    cabbage
For 500ml (1 pint, 2½ cups) water:
    3 fresh chillis
    30ml (2 tablespoons) rice wine
    30ml (2 tablespoons) sea salt
    10ml (2 teaspoons) Sichuan
        peppercorns
6 slices ginger
1 garlic clove, sliced

Wash and trim all the vegetables and
cut where necessary into bite-sized
pieces. Soak in cold boiled water for 2
hours. Meanwhile slice the chillis. Mix
the rice wine, sea salt and peppercorns with 500ml (1 pint, 2½ cups)
water in a glass or china bowl. Add the
chillis, ginger and garlic. Drain the
vegetables and put into the bowl.
There should be enough vegetables
to pack tightly. Lay on a small plate to
hold them under the water and cover
the bowl with cling-wrap. Keep at
room temperature for 2 days, then put
in the refrigerator for 2 days.
   Eat after 4 days.

Shacha (southern fire-pot)

苍式火煱

75g (3 oz) dried rice noodles
500g (1 lb) beef fillet
150g (5 oz) raw prawns, shelled
500g (1 lb) boned chicken breast
250g (8 oz) turbot
1kg (2 lb) green vegetable (spinach, lettuce,
    watercress, etc.)
2 litres (3 pints, 2 quarts) good stock
oil for deep frying
raw eggs
shachajiang
soy sauce

Cut the rice noodles in half and deep-fry for 2 minutes. Drain well and put on a serving plate. Cut the beef (shown above in a heart-shape) into paper-thin slices and arrange on a plate. Garnish to taste. De-vein the prawns, flatten them with the flat of a knife and arrange on a plate (these are shown as bird shapes). Slice the chicken very thinly and lay on a plate. Divide the turbot (shown as 'eagles') into very thin slices and arrange on another plate. (Vary the designs to your own taste.) Wash and tear the green vegetables into small pieces. Put on two plates. Have ready the boiling soup in the centre of the table over a table stove. Arrange the plates round it. Give each diner a raw egg to mix with *shachajiang* and soy sauce (to taste) in his bowl. When the meal starts each diner dips a piece of meat or fish into the stock and dips it in his sauce before eating.

When the meat and fish are finished put the vegetables and rice noodles into the pot and serve as a soup.

Plum Blossom Hotpot

梅花火煱

12 pork meatballs (see page 40)
200g (7 oz) chicken breast, without bones
2 spring onions
2 slices ginger
60ml (4 tablespoons) oil
1 stuffed egg omelette (see page 173)
250g (8 oz) Cantonese roast pork
1 litre (2 pints, 5 cups) boiling stock
74 fish balls (bought)
25g (1 oz) beansprouts, blanched

Make the pork meatballs according to the recipe on page 40. Fry in 30ml (2 tablespoons) oil until brown on all sides, then add 250ml (½ pint, 1¼ cups) water and simmer for 15 minutes. Put on one side. Cut the chicken breast into 2cm (1-inch) cubes. Heat 15ml (1 tablespoon) oil and stir-fry the onion and ginger. Then add the chicken and stir-fry 5 minutes. Make the stuffed omelette as described on page 173. Steam for 20 minutes, then cut into slices. Cut the Cantonese pork into slices.

Have ready a centre table hot-plate (or use an electric hotpot). Arrange the meatballs, chicken, omelette slices, roast pork, fish balls and bean sprouts in a casserole, and pour in the boiling stock. Bring the pot to the table and put it on the hot-plate. When it re-boils, serve.

Vegetarian Duckling

茄醬素鴨

3 sheets dried beancurd
30ml (2 tablespoons) sesame oil
30ml (2 tablespoons) soy sauce
15ml (1 tablespoon) cornflour
oil for deep frying

Soak the beancurd sheets in warm water until soft. Then pat dry and paint each sheet with a mixture of sesame oil, soy sauce and cornflour. Lay one on top of the other and fold them all into a square. Steam for 30 minutes. Then heat the oil over a moderate heat and deep-fry the beancurd skin packet for 30 seconds. Leave until cold, then cut into slices. Serve with Chinese chilli sauce, or tomato ketchup as a dip.

Chinese Leaves with Crab Sauce

蟹肉
焗白菜

500g (1 lb) Chinese leaves
1 spring onion
30ml (2 tablespoons) cornflour
12g (½ oz) lard
2 slices ginger
60g (2½ oz) crab meat
150ml (¼ pint, ⅔ cup) stock
150ml (¼ pint, ⅔ cup) milk
salt and pepper to taste

Wash the cabbage and cut into shreds. Chop the spring onion. Mix the cornflour with 45ml (3 tablespoons) water.

Melt the lard and stir-fry the onion and ginger. Then remove the ginger and add the cabbage. Stir-fry for about 3 minutes, then mix in the crab meat. Continue stir-frying for another minute before pouring in the stock and milk. Bring to the boil and adjust the seasoning. Thicken with the cornflour paste. Tip into a fire-proof dish and put under the grill to brown on top. Serve hot.

Steamed Rice with Chicken and Chinese Sausage

芥蘭腊味飯

2 Chinese sausages
30ml (2 tablespoons) rice wine
2 spring onions, chopped
300g (10 oz) roast chicken (leg)
2 slices ginger
250g (8 oz) choisam
450g (1 lb) rice
900ml (1½ pints, 3¾ cups)
　　stock
45ml (3 tablespoons) oil
2ml (½ teaspoon) salt

Slice the sausages and put them with 15ml (1 tablespoon) rice wine in a small bowl. Add half the chopped onion. Chop the chicken into bite-sized pieces and put it with the remaining rice wine and spring onion into a bowl. Add the ginger. Wash and trim the *choisam* and cut into 5cm (2-inch) lengths. Wash the rice thoroughly.

Steam the sausage and chicken for about 10 minutes. Cook the rice with the stock in a covered pan for 20 minutes. Meanwhile stir-fry the *choisam* in the oil with the salt for about 3 minutes. When the rice is cooked put the sausage, chicken and *choisam* on top of the rice, and pour in their cooking juices. Cover and cook over a *very low* heat for another 10 minutes. Serve hot.

Cauliflower and Pork Congee

菜花玉米粥

150g (5 oz) minced pork
5ml (1 teaspoon) soy sauce
5ml (1 teaspoon) rice
2ml (½ teaspoon) salt
250g (8 oz) cauliflower
300g (10 oz) rice
1 spring onion
3.5 litres (6 pints, 3 quarts) stock
　　or water
60ml (4 tablespoons) oil
30ml (2 tablespoons) peas

Marinate the pork with the soy sauce, rice wine and salt. Wash, and cut the cauliflower into florets. Wash the rice thoroughly. Chop the spring onion into 1cm (½-inch) lengths.

Put the rice on to boil with the stock or water. Heat the oil and stir-fry the spring onion. Add the pork and stir-fry for about 3 minutes. Then add the peas and cauliflower and continue stir-frying for another 2 minutes. After the rice has cooked for 25 minutes stir in the pork, peas and cauliflower and continue cooking for another 15 minutes. Check the seasoning and serve.

213

Deep-fried Bean Balls

豆沙高麗肉

150g (5 oz) red-bean paste (bought)
1 egg
150g (5 oz) flour
125g (4 oz) icing sugar
oil for deep frying

Roll the red-bean paste into small balls the size of cherries. Cover with cling-wrap and put into the refrigerator overnight. The next day mix the egg, flour and 150ml (¼ pint, ⅔ cup) water into a batter. Heat the oil to very hot. Dip each ball of red-bean paste into the batter, then drop into the hot oil. Deep-fry until golden brown. Lift out, drain and roll in the sugar before serving.

Four-shreds Spring Rolls

四絲春捲

200g (7 oz) lean pork
15ml (1 tablespoon) soy sauce
5ml (1 teaspoon) rice wine
5ml (1 teaspoon) salt
3 dried mushrooms
250g (8 oz) Chinese cabbage
14 spring onions
14 spring roll skins (bought)
oil for deep frying

Cut the pork into matchstick shreds and marinate with 5ml (1 teaspoon) soy sauce, the rice wine and a pinch of salt. Soak the mushrooms in warm water for 30 minutes, then discard the hard stalks and cut the caps into shreds. Trim, wash and shred the Chinese cabbage. Trim the spring onions into 6cm (2½-inch) lengths.

Heat 45ml (3 tablespoons) oil and stir-fry the mushrooms. Add the pork and stir-fry until it changes colour. Lift out and clean the pan. Heat 30ml (2 tablespoons) oil and stir-fry the Chinese cabbage for 2 minutes. Add in the mushrooms, pork and 10ml (2 teaspoons) soy sauce and continue stir-frying until the Chinese cabbage is cooked. Remove and leave to cool.

Arrange about 30ml (2 tablespoons) of the pork mixture in the centre of each spring roll skin. Lay one or two onion lengths on top, then fold in and roll up the spring roll skin. Heat the oil and deep-fry the spring rolls, a few at a time, over a moderate heat. When they are all cooked raise the temperature and re-fry until they are a dark golden brown. Lift out, drain and serve.

Sweet Congee with Rice Balls

酒 釀 圓 子

75g (3 oz) glutinous rice
75g (3 oz) glutinous rice flour
25g (1 oz) glacé cherries
sugar to taste

Soak the rice in cold water for 3 hours. Then rinse and put into 1.5 litres (2⅓ pints, 6 cups) water and boil for 1 hour. Towards the end of the cooking make the rice balls by mixing the rice flour with 55ml (3½ tablespoons, ¼ cup) water and kneading into a smooth paste. Shape into small balls the size of a thumb nail. When the rice is cooked drop the balls into the pan and continue boiling until they rise to the surface. Add the cherries and sugar to taste before serving.

Silver Ears with Pineapple

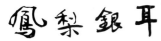

10 dried red dates
12g (½ oz) silver ears
1 small can pineapple
125g (4 oz) crystal sugar

Soak the dates for 3 hours in cold water, then rinse well, stone and drain. Soak the silver ears for 30 minutes in hot water, then rinse and cut away any yellow or coarse bits. Cut the pineapple into bite-sized chunks.

Boil the dates gently in 1.5 litres (2⅓ pints, 6 cups) water for 30 minutes. Then add the silver ears and sugar and simmer for 1 hour. Add the pineapple chunks and cook for another 5 minutes. Check to see it is sweet enough and serve. Or allow to cool and chill before serving.